ROMANTICISM

Author: Léon Rosenthal

Layout:
Baseline Co. Ltd,
District 3, Ho Chi Minh City
Vietnam

ISBN: 978-1-68325-937-4

Printed in

Léon Rosenthal

ROMANTICISM

Emotion, imagination, and the power of nature

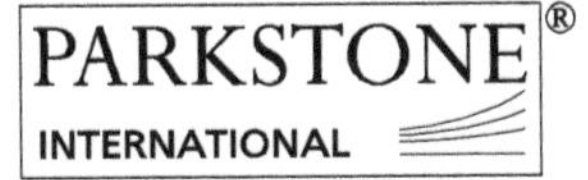

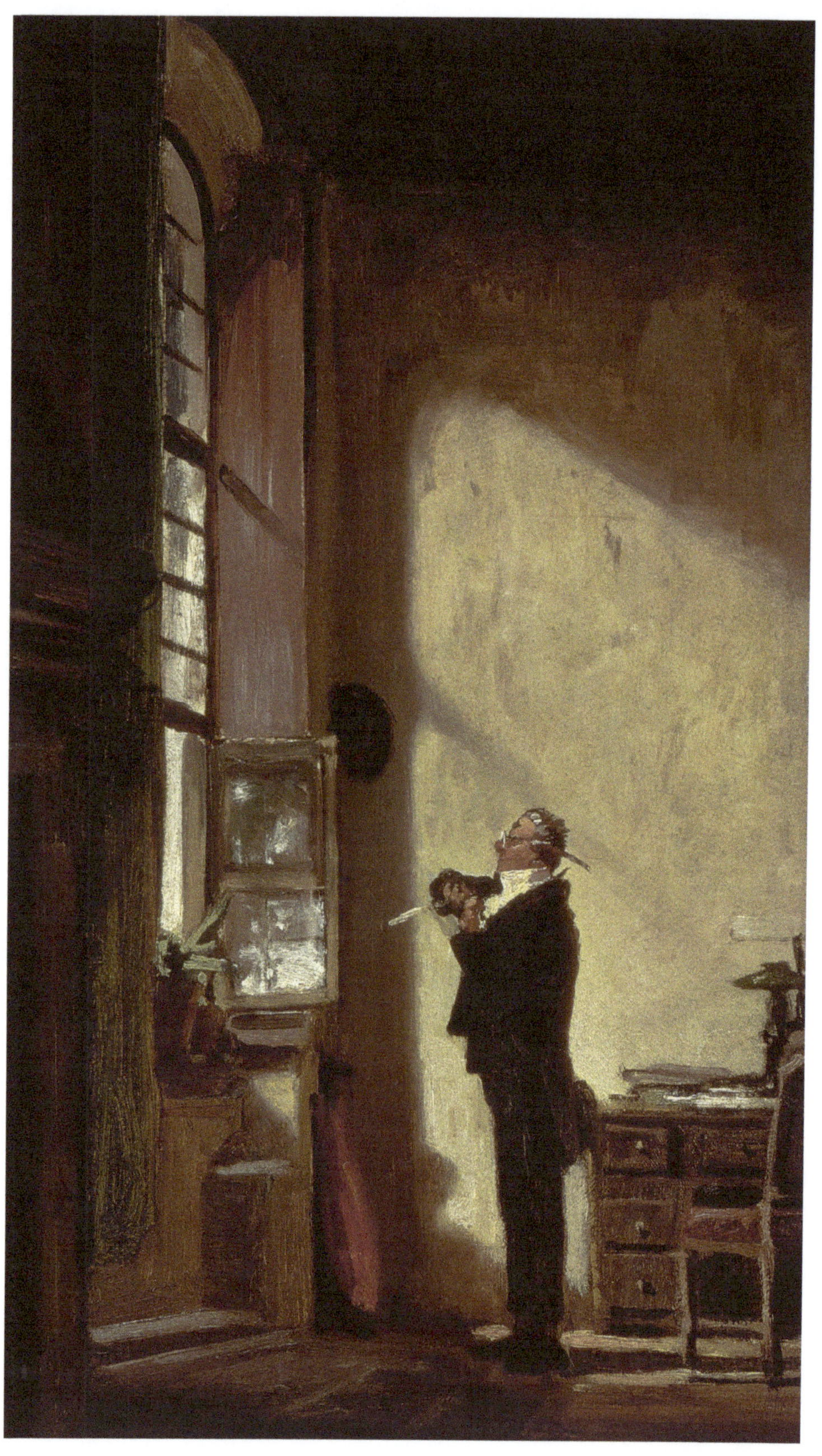

CONTENTS

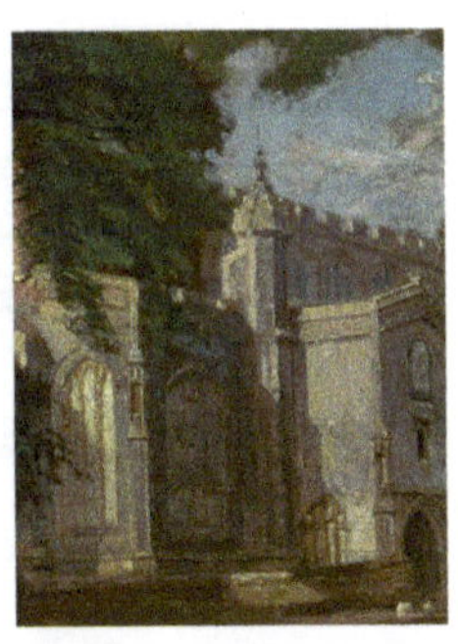

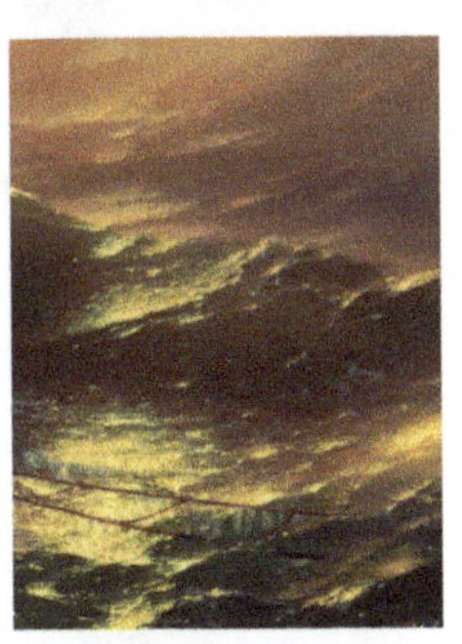

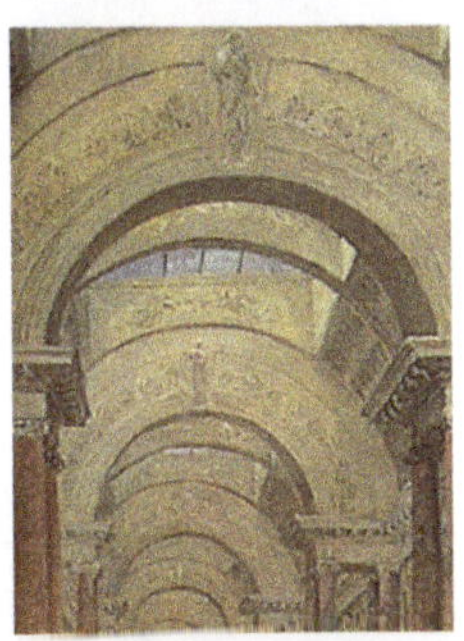

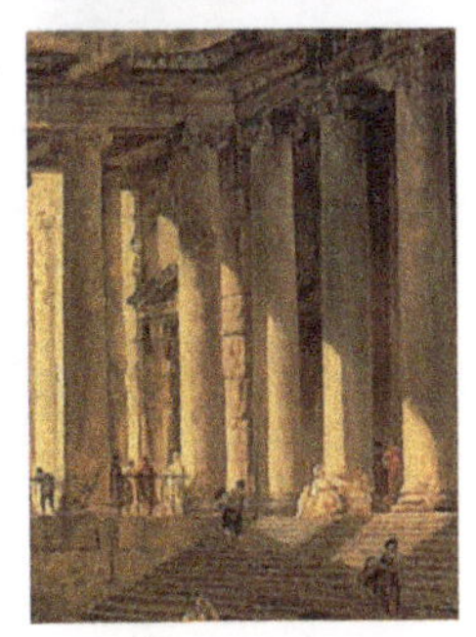

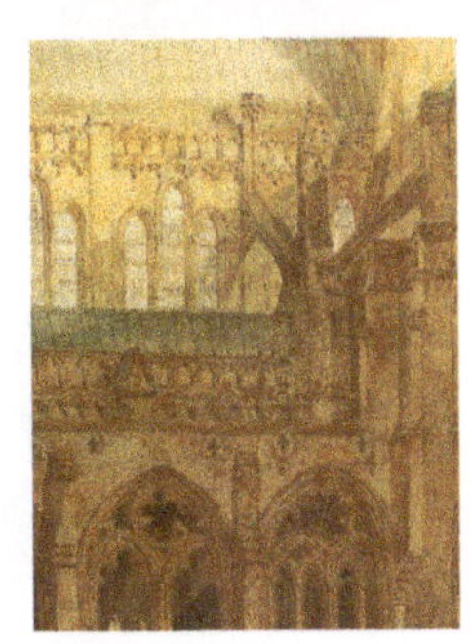

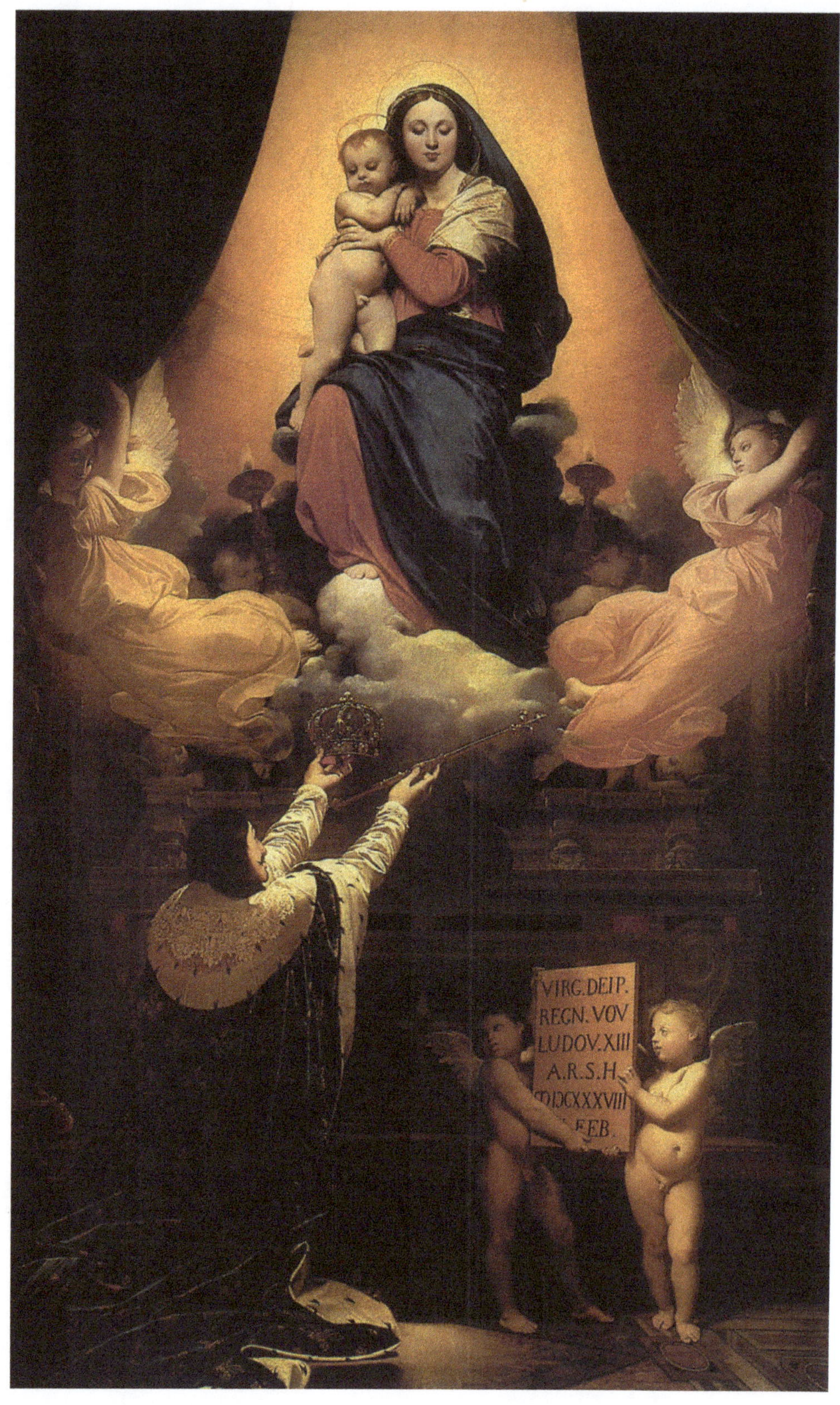
VIRG. DEIP.
REGN. VOV
LUDOV. XIII
A.R.S.H.
ↃIↃCXXXVIII
FEB.

The Precursors of Romanticism

The Romantic Age! Youth, ardour, a generous faith in art, excessive passions; amongst fevers, exaggerations, errors, it was a period really full of ideas, personalities and works.

Literary Romanticism has been subject to great arguments and violent controversy, particularly because it was considered to be responsible for divisive religious, political or social tendencies. Romantic art received less attention, perhaps because it seemed comparatively unimportant. However, it is possible to dissociate the two movements. They were linked not because of personal friendships developing by chance between a few painters and writers but because those movements, in their different ways, share in the same origin. Born from a common mindset,

they had developed in the same atmosphere. There was a Romantic generation the members of which applied their minds to literature and the arts as well as to science, philosophy, politics or industry – in fact to all the forms of activity to which their minds could possibly be applied.

The canons of Romanticism were first formulated in Germany at the end of the eighteenth century. As early as 1770 and 1780 representatives of *Sturm und Drang*, a movement both literary and political, meaning literally 'storm and stress', were rebelling against the Enlightenment and its values. Friedrich von Schiller and Johann Wolfgang von Goethe were amongst the followers of *Sturm und Drang*, who made a religion of individualism and nature as advocated by Jean-Jacques Rousseau in the middle of the eighteenth century. However, despite that wave of protest the rejection of classical rules was only partial. *Sturm und Drang* turned its back on classical traditions and literary conventions but its canons of beauty were still based on Antiquity and prescribed the perfection and harmony of forms. Classicism was totally rejected as a whole by the intellectuals contributing to the journal

▲ **Carl Spitzweg**,
The Writer, 19th century.
Oil on canvas.
Kunsthaus, Munich.

◀ **Jean-Auguste-Dominique Ingres**,
The Vow of Louis XIII, 1824.
Oil on canvas, 421 x 262 cm.
Cathédrale Notre-Dame, Montauban.

Athenaeum, amongst whom were Wilhelm von Schelling and Novalis representing the 'Iena Romantics' group. In contrast with earlier values they put an emphasis on the feeling of infinity, mysticism and the expression of irrationality.

In Ireland, the Philosophical Enquiry into the *Origin of our Ideas of the Sublime and the Beautiful* by Edmund Burke, published in 1756, developed the Romantic vision of nature. In Burke's remarks on painting, one notes the same tendency through "the painting of the sublime" on the one hand and the "mysticism of landscapes" on the other, clearly exemplified by the works of Caspar David Friedrich. In 1762, James McPherson's English translation of Poems of Ossian became a reference for Romanticism. Allegedly attributed to a Scottish bard of the third century, the origins of the book are mysterious but it appealed to the collective imagination and plunged its readers into the depths of their dreams.

Thus the European literature of the eighteenth century paved the way for Romanticism, but it is in the art of the nineteenth century, particularly in France, that it reached its zenith. French art at the time formed an imposing structure whose magnificent order reflected the heroic times that had built it. A fanatical admiration for Greco-Roman Antiquity was still defended. Art's only goal seemed to be to revive the inspiration and methods of that blessed time, which alone had managed to bring pure, serene and ideal beauty out of humanity. But Antiquity could appear multi-faced depending on the eyes and predispositions of its admirers: by turn it could be solemn, pleasant, frivolous, noble, generous or depraved. When men imagined it tense, stiff, stilted and raised towards inaccessible peaks they projected their own genius onto it. Through Socrates, Romulus and Leonidas they glorified their own century. They praised the human figure, powerful bodies with wide chests, regular facial features, strong contours, refined drawing, vivid colours devoid of ornaments, subordinated nature reduced to the passive role of décor. Everything echoed the tendencies of generations galvanised first by their passion for freedom and then for glory. Bare and stilted statues, devoid of accentuation, appealed to eyes that could not stand the graces of the eighteenth century. Palaces, temples and commemorative monuments tried to convey the majesty of that time through plain, solid and large structures drawing on Vitruve's repertoire. Inside the buildings, mahogany furniture followed heavy architectural patterns and decorations included chiselled noble copperware, solemn chandeliers and grandfather clocks, wall coverings adorned with large geometrical patterns in which gold, green and Etruscan red were associated, composed austere and simple harmonies designed for a new and rather unrefined society that had forgotten the gentle way of life. It was an artificial but perfectly adequate setting whose consistency was quite remarkable and particularly striking when contrasted with the

Jean-Baptiste Mallet, ▶
Gothic Bathroom, 1810.
Oil on canvas, 40.5 x 32.5 cm.
Château-Musée de Dieppe, Dieppe.

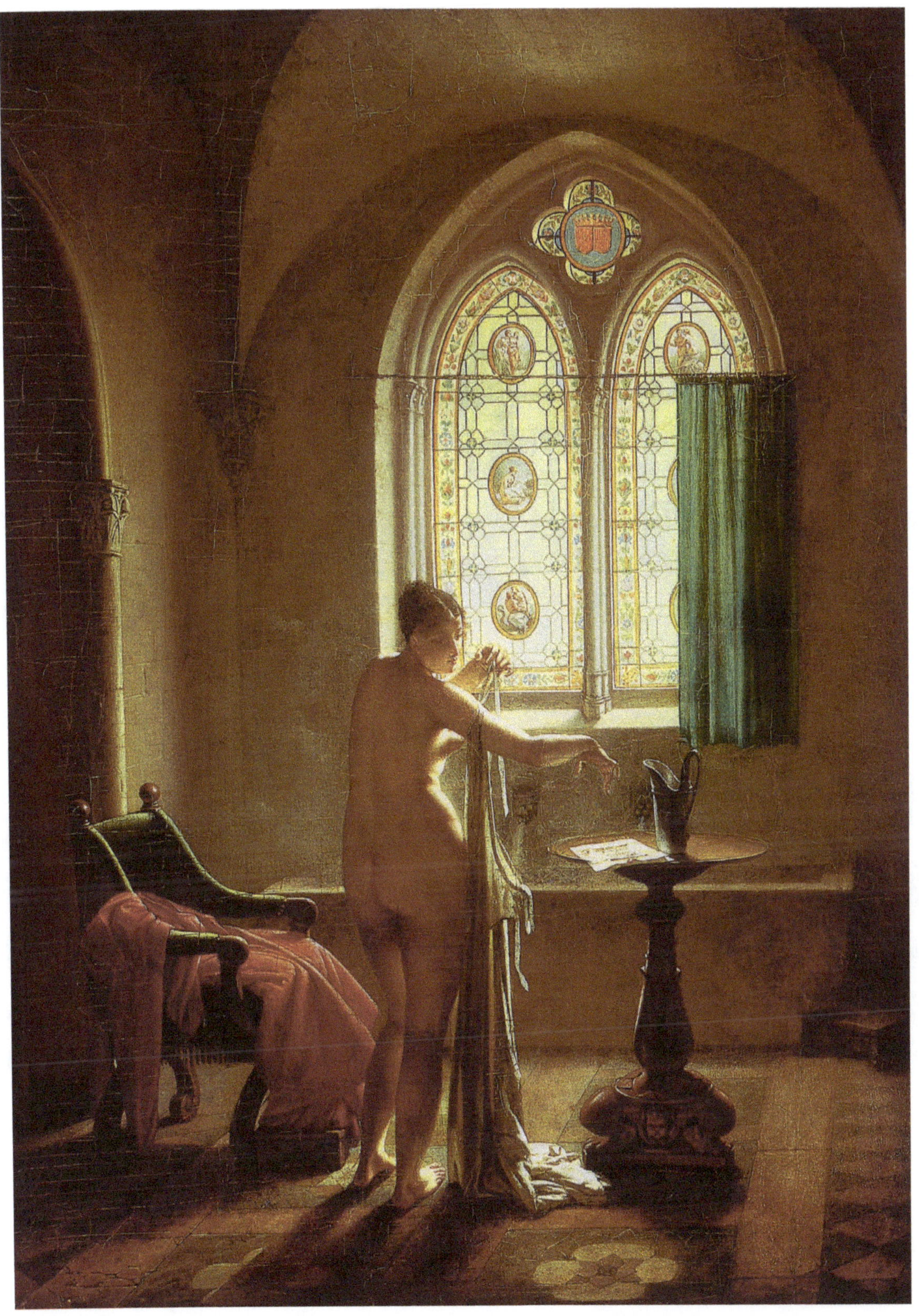

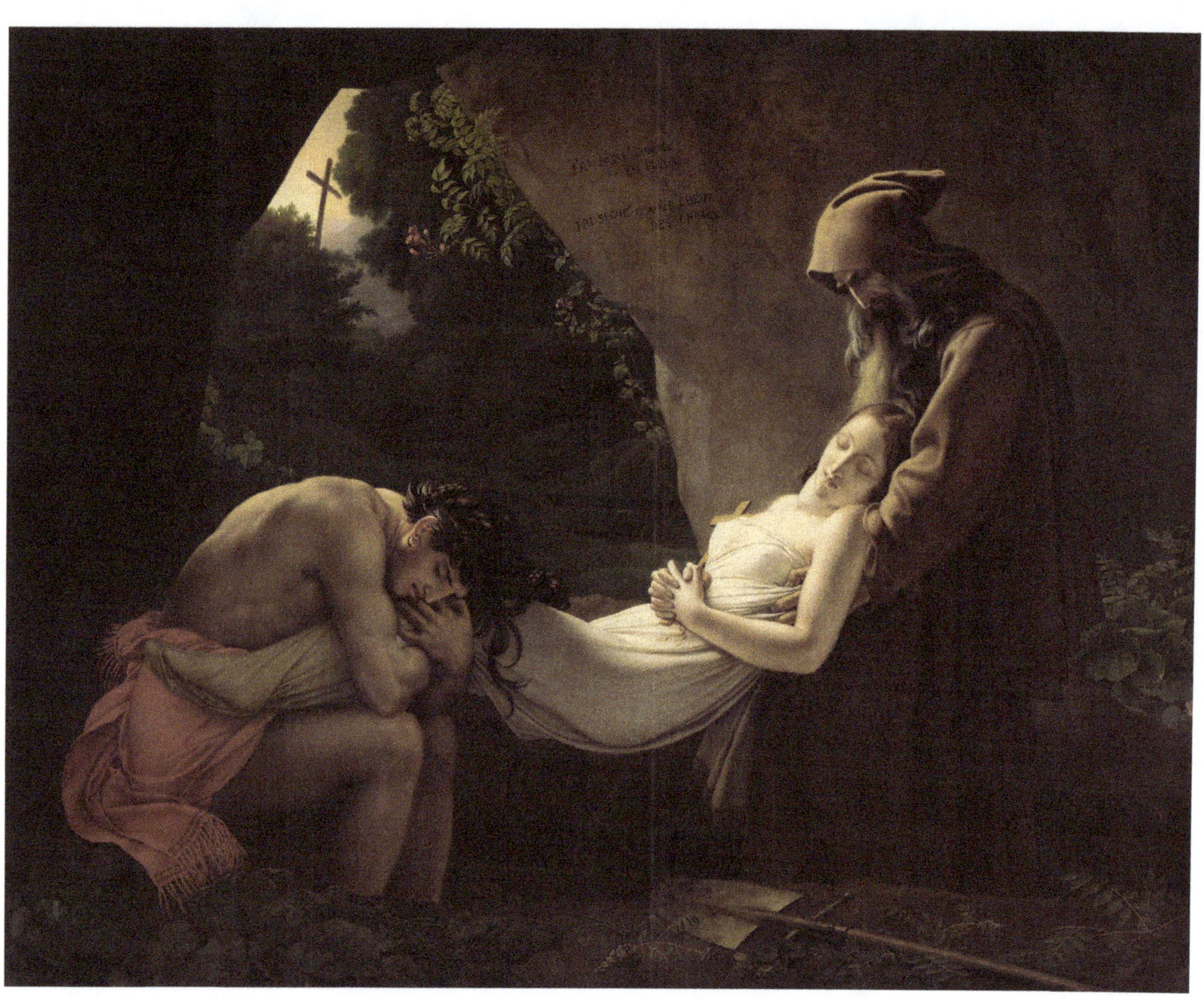

disorder of the following period. The brilliance of that style, though it was soon to be tarnished, was nevertheless magnificent. At the same time that France provided politics, sciences and the army with men of genius or great talent, she also supplied the arts with an élite, a whole host of stars.

If we put aside our modern prejudices we can understand the pride with which people of the time talked of the "French School". Around David, the leader, there were painters like Girodet, Gérard, Guérin, Gros and Proudhon. Most of these masters were still active when the Empire collapsed, and they had trained students whose works had started to appear. Based on a strong doctrine illustrated by exemplary works, the French School was well on course to carry on its glorious career.

However, it was fragile as was the Empire itself and complex forces were at work to try and destroy it despite its triumphant appearances. Strangely enough, the French School imposed a precise discipline on artists at the very time when the Revolution was breaking the social codes and teaching individuals that their originality, boldness and energy could get them where they wanted in society. In some it shook up instincts of generosity that had been put to sleep by systematic minds; to others, who had

◀ **Anne-Louis Girodet de Roucy**, called **Girodet-Trioson**, *The Entombment of Atala*, 1808.
Oil on canvas, 207 x 267 cm.
Musée du Louvre, Paris.

been repressing desires of wealth, pleasure and brilliance, it offered a multitude of exciting opportunities and made them seek new and diverse acquaintances and lifestyles. Hypnotised by a conventional view of Antiquity, David had ignored the past totally until the revolutionary crisis rekindled his interest in history. As a child Michelet, wild with enthusiasm, would pace up and down the rooms of the Musée des Monuments Français (Museum of French Monuments) where Lenoir, who founded the museum with the stone works he saved from the violent fury of the Revolution, displayed several centuries of history. A certain image of France started to be outlined, albeit vague and pale at first, and the troubadour style foreshadowed the development of a new kind of spirit.

At the same time there arose an interest in churches and cathedrals, buildings which had been previously looked down upon. In 1802 Chateaubriand published *Genius of Christianity*, which echoed the hopes of a whole generation. He claimed in it that religious inspiration was superior to all others. Elsewhere, the Empire kept silent whilst economic activity slowed down and young men were decimated in a state permanently at war, which caused a feeling of weariness. The influence of Rousseau deepened in this climate, manifest in Sénancour's 1804 telling of *Obermann*'s dark destiny, who alone in the Alps sought consolation in nature. So despite appearing arrogant the general atmosphere tended towards the dissolution of the French School. But it faced more direct assaults from within the artistic world itself.

David had established himself through total rebellion against the eighteenth century. He disowned his masters and, with them, the whole inheritance of traditions accumulated since the Renaissance, preferring antique style models and casting. In 1793 the Louvre Museum opened to the public. Victories over Italy and Flanders allowed it soon to be filled with masterpieces whilst a growing fancy of collectors for Dutch paintings became quite noticeable.

At the heart of the French School, amongst its protagonists and most famous masters, a new and transformed future was in preparation, and the people of the time got a partial sense of it. They did not realise that *The Death of Marat*, *The Coronation* or the multiplication of portraits helped artists in liberating themselves, but they feared Gros's action. A shy man, whose most sincere desire would have been to become the loyal right-hand man of David, he was driven by an internal force seemingly in spite of himself. Unwillingly, he carried the truths that were about to blossom. *Napoleon at Jaffa* was more than the preface to Romanticism. It asserted the joy of painting as well as a research into characterisation, movement and liveliness, to which orientalism and a picturesque quality were added. This famous painting that young people kept referring to was not an exceptional phenomenon, however. The whole of Gros's work, his huge paintings, his portraits, sketches and watercolours, developed a whole programme: the supremacy of colour, the study of places and races, an interest in animals and particularly the big cats. National history was represented by the

Visit of *Charles V and François I at Saint-Denis*; he thought of *Othello* and *Ugolin* in 1804 and the posthumous portrait of Lucien Bonaparte's wife is shrouded in a modern kind of melancholy.

Ingres's works like *Jupiter and Thetis* – still amazing to us nowadays – were painted at the time of David's supremacy and are full of inspiration, sensitivity and expressive moods that were totally new. Among so many docile artists Ingres showed an untameable independence; he had broken off with David and wanted to 'become an innovator, have his works imprinted with a character unknown' before him. Acquaintance with the Italian primitives had polished his subtle drawing. He was one of the first to acknowledge their art as he was also the first to consider Greek vases. He would feed his genius with ideas from all sorts of areas: classical Antiquity, history, poetry, the reality of the time and oriental countries. He did not look down on colour, adored Titian and, being versatile, nervous, changing his style from one painting to the other, he would sometimes invent sharp harmonies and precious dissonances. With an implacable precision but also infinite suppleness his lines shrouded pure but non abstract shapes in which concentrated fieriness and a sensual love for beauty were visible. He who painted Fingal's fantasy paradise, Thetis' wavy body, and surrounded the dreamy Madame de Sénones with a floating languid atmosphere was

Édouard Cibot, ▶
Anne Boleyn in the Tower, 1835.
Oil on canvas, 162 x 129 cm.
Musée Rolin, Autun.

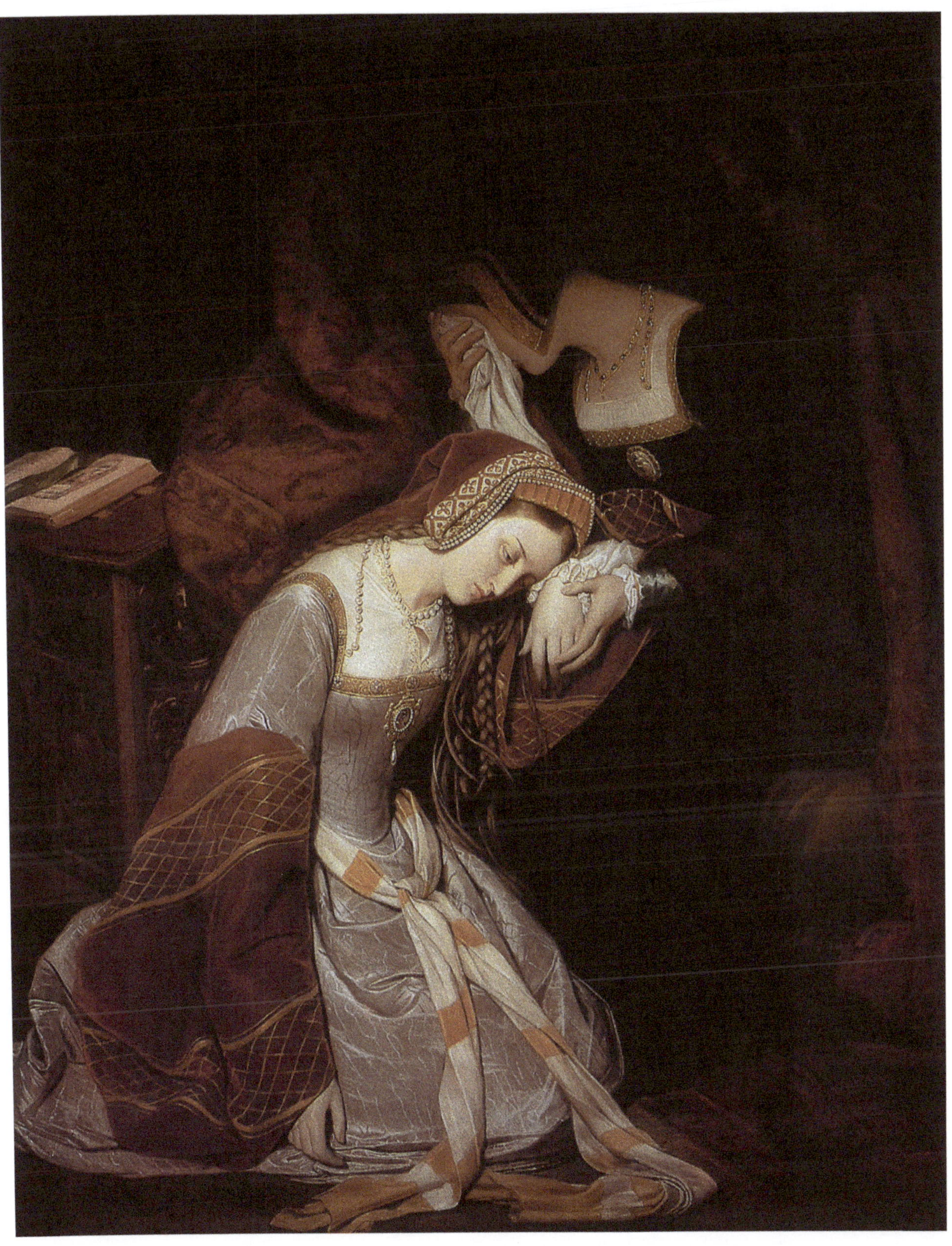

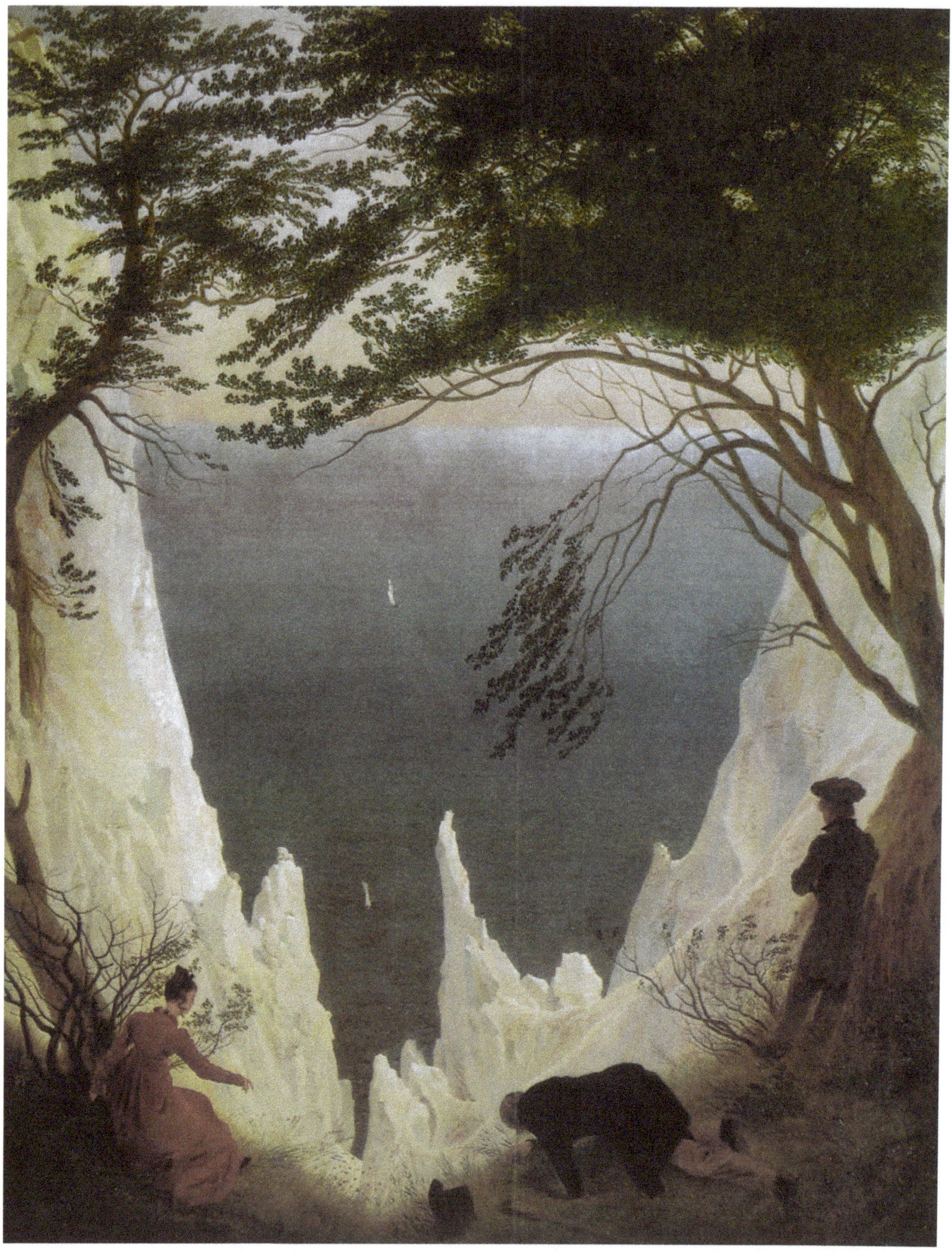

a pre-Romantic in his own way, like Gros, and in fact more exceptional and more modern than the latter. His power was not yet recognised, though. People were sensitive to a charm that was seen as ineffable but feared the technical examples that he set. It was believed that he drew badly because he was not superstitious about the outline. On bluish paper he would use charcoal and chalk to bring out volumes and shroud synthetic and quivering shapes in space. He kept a love for graces in an heroic age but with a penetrating fieriness unknown to the eighteenth century, and he added a sense of worry to it that dragged him away from the past and made him closer to us.

Sculpture developed in a more balanced way. It was obsessed by a passion for heroic ideals more than any other form of art. Houdon continued to flourish, restating his profound genius with a bust of Napoleon.

A few signs of something about to be born were also visible in architecture. The emperor's official architects, Percier and Fontaine, were touched by the smiles of the Italian Renaissance.

So at a time when it was believed that the arts had taken a definite direction and found fixed shapes, some forces were at work preparing for an evolution that was waiting to happen. Those forces were complex and paradoxical in many

◄ **Caspar David Friedrich,**
Chalk Cliffs on Rügen, 1818-1819.
Oil on canvas, 90 x 70 cm.
Museum Oskar Reinhart am Stadtgarten, Winterthur.

ways. Some wished for the supremacy of reality whilst others praised imagination and dreams. None of these tendencies gave way but their fate would be determined by future events. If the Empire had grown stronger and had settled in a stable order, minds would have relaxed gradually; a calm, healthy and balanced kind of art would probably have developed ensuring the triumph of realism. But on the contrary, if a storm was to burst out, a period of crisis would consequently start in which disoriented artists would listen to their sensitivity and nerves rather than rationality: that would mark the triumph of Romanticism.

It turned out to be a storm and a most terrible one. The fall of the Empire, the invasion of the country and the return of the Bourbons shook France deeply, and it was left feeling humiliated and hurt. From then on, neither religion, politics nor any position in society could offer a secure shelter. The *mal du siècle* became exacerbated. Helpless men turned in on themselves; they looked into their own minds in search of the laws at work behind their actions. They soared painfully on the uncertain paths of liberty, guided by their feelings and not by logic. At that time England, from which France had been cut off because of war, recreated the contacts initiated by Voltaire in the eighteenth century. France had already turned to Germany, and the influence of Germanic countries occurred precisely in the way that Madame de Staël had indicated with great lucidity: Goethe, Schiller, Shakespeare, Walter Scott, Constable, Lawrence and Beethoven came to feed the longings of an anxious generation. This is how Romantic times started.

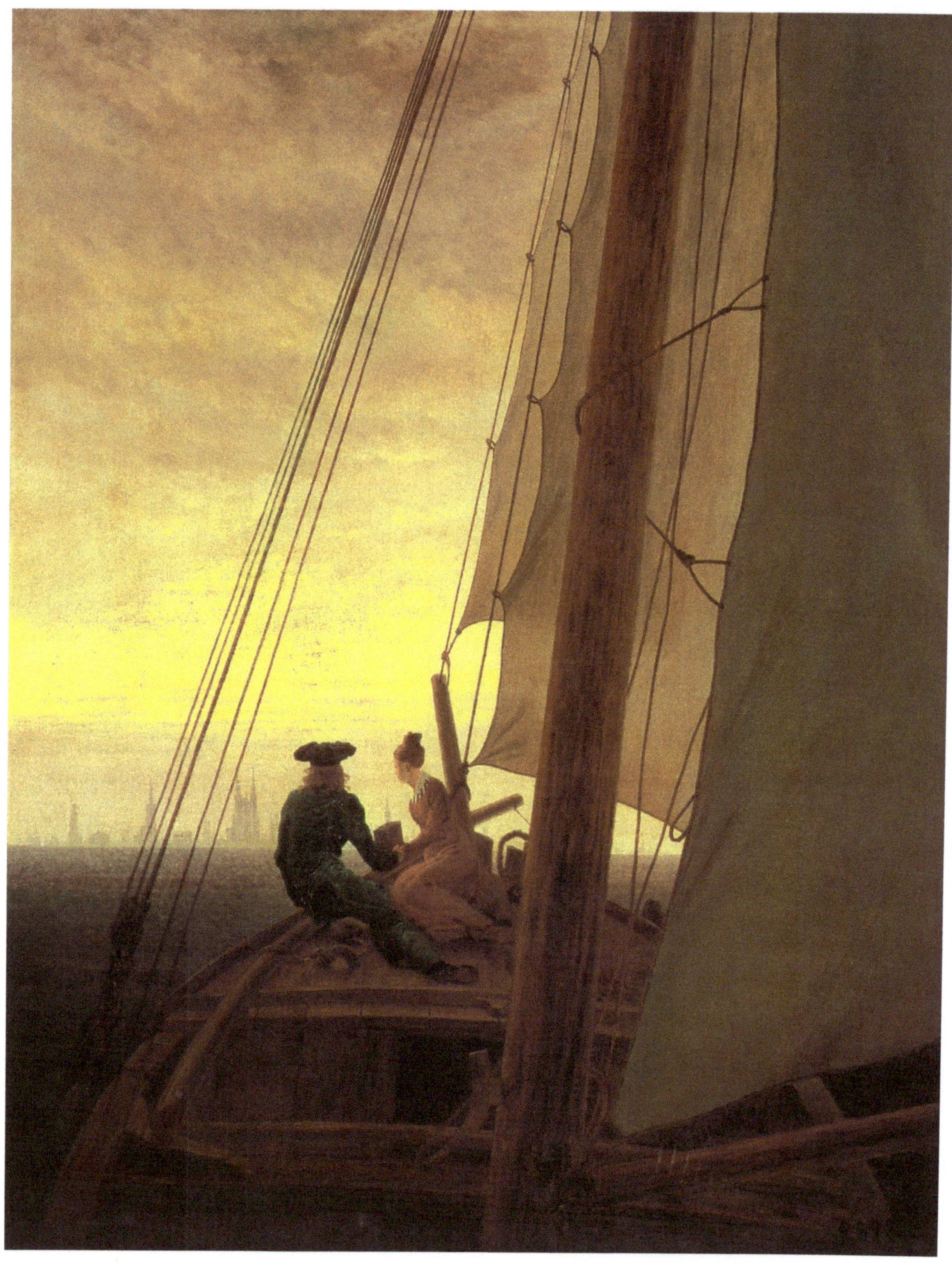

The Romantic Period

At the Exhibition of 1817, the first to take place after the Restoration, the public did not notice any signs of change. Despite David's exile, the same masters were present defending the same ideas. Beside them there were some young people, their students and followers, supporting the cause.

No doubt it was wished that politics had not imposed or suggested topics remote from the artistic mission such as historical anecdotes or religious themes. Gérard had painted the *Entry of Henri IV into Paris* in the same way that he had celebrated the 10th August in the past. There were also signs of weariness; with shy audacity some artists had created scenes with a dramatic quality or tinged with light effects. In fact, there was nothing there to write home about. The young Horace Vernet displayed a large picturesque painting with his *Battle of Las Navas de Tolosa* but that was an isolated case; the Grand Condé by David d'Angers triggered some curiosity but without raising fears.

◀ **Caspar David Friedrich**,
On the Sailing Boat, 1818-1820.
Oil on canvas, 71 x 56 cm.
The State Hermitage Museum, St Petersburg.

However, fervent, anxious and nervous young people questioned and looked for the future in studios or at the Louvre at that very time. They sensed, without understanding the exact reasons for it, that life was now to be found outside the formulae that had ensured the glory of French art for half a century. There had been a soul lying in these tried and tested formulae which was no longer shared by these young people. Some historic and respectable academic rules were still in use, but outdated. Famous professors no longer had control over these young people. They fumbled for new means of expression or, as sometimes happens in such situations, they would temporarily seek guidance from a friend who seemed momentarily inspired.

At the Exhibition of 1819 latent ideas suddenly appeared, revealing themselves in the scandal of *The Raft of the Medusa*. It was a huge painting whose dimensions alone were a challenge, and it imposed authority in itself even upon those who were distressed by it. No doubt that the battle had started. In that painting, Géricault rejected everything that the French School had stood for: the hierarchy of genres (as he treated a news item like an epic), ideal beauty, the supremacy of drawing, apparent finish, balanced order and serenity.

That vehemently powerful work claimed the joy of painting, the rights of movement, drama, and life. Beyond David's canon, it was based on principles from the past and strengthened by the tradition it had returned to, whilst at the same time announcing a free form of art. Critics moaned and were disturbed by the multiplication of mundane and religious topics, but young people praised Géricault and saw in him their new leader. He still had a natural penchant for the realist epic that few shared, but he set an example for all and gave them the courage to assert themselves.

Those around him, and in particular the young Delacroix, were attracted by his work and could see something special in it. His drawings, gouaches and watercolours often confirmed what Gros had intuitively discovered, but at the same time he pioneered techniques in different fields. Invented in 1796, lithography had only produced uncertain and imperfect outcomes; Géricault took it up and, with remarkable confidence, revealed its full potential. Lithography would have been inadequate for David and his students, who would have found it too greasy, supple, colourful and sometimes excessive, but it turned out to be perfectly suitable for the new generation.

Géricault's action was profound and long lasting though he did not show work in public again after the Medusa. He did not take part in the Exhibition of 1822 and died at the beginning of 1824. Before Géricault's death, Eugène Delacroix had taken up his torch. Dante and Virgil was showed at the Exhibition of 1822 and made him famous. Close to him were artists like Bonington, Champmartin, Sigalon, Camille Roqueplan, Ary Scheffer and Achille Devéria, some of whom achieved enduring fame.

At the Exhibition of 1824 scattered signs of change had turned into a generalised movement in which was at stake the whole direction that art was to take. The Romantics flocked together. Besides Bonington, Copley Fielding, Constable and Lawrence came to display their works at the Exhibition as if they wanted to support the avant-garde. Facing such attacks and desertion, the French School resisted; it would not let go and the fight turned out to be much harder for artists than writers. Victor Hugo and his emulators faced mediocre writers with worn out, passé formulae who opposed them with insults and mockery but not with powerful works. However, the School which the young artists had decided to destroy was too recent, and the fits of enthusiasm that it had produced were only just past. Girodet was still very successful with *Pygmalion* at the Exhibition of 1819, but time was not on the School's side and nobody had David's authority or the productivity needed either to impose discipline on the young or to stimulate them and give them confidence in proven doctrines. A figure to lead the resistance was looked for, and Ingres was called on for help.

At the time he was blacklisted. *La Grande Odalisque*, on display beside Roger delivering *Angelica* at the Exhibition of 1819, had been accused of multiple flaws and seen as directing art backwards to its primitive age, though avant-garde artists appreciated his work. At the Exhibition of 1824, however, The *Vow of Louis XIII* created a sudden

Théodore Géricault, ▶
The Raft of the Medusa, 1819.
Oil on canvas, 491 x 716 cm.
Musée du Louvre, Paris.

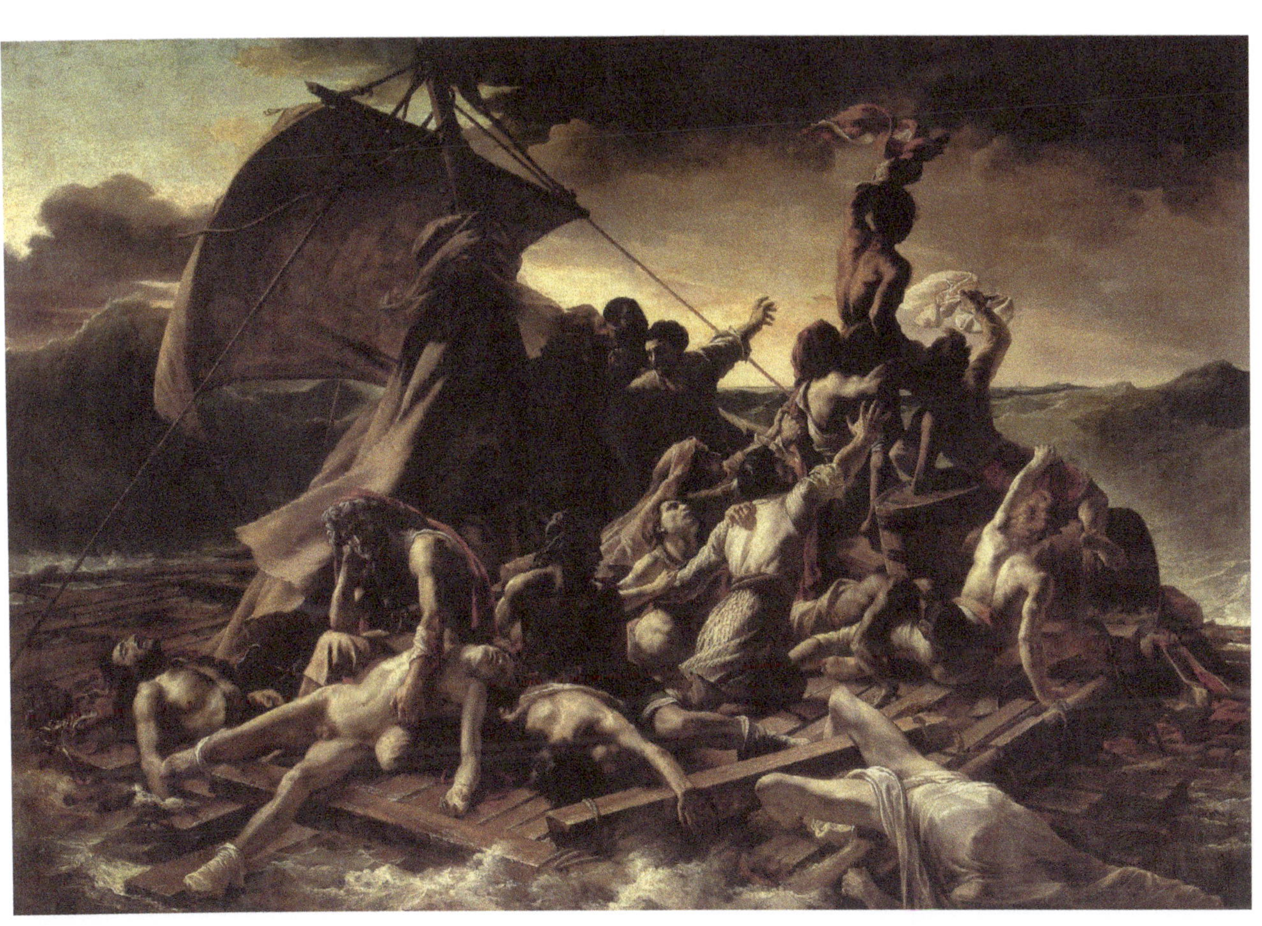

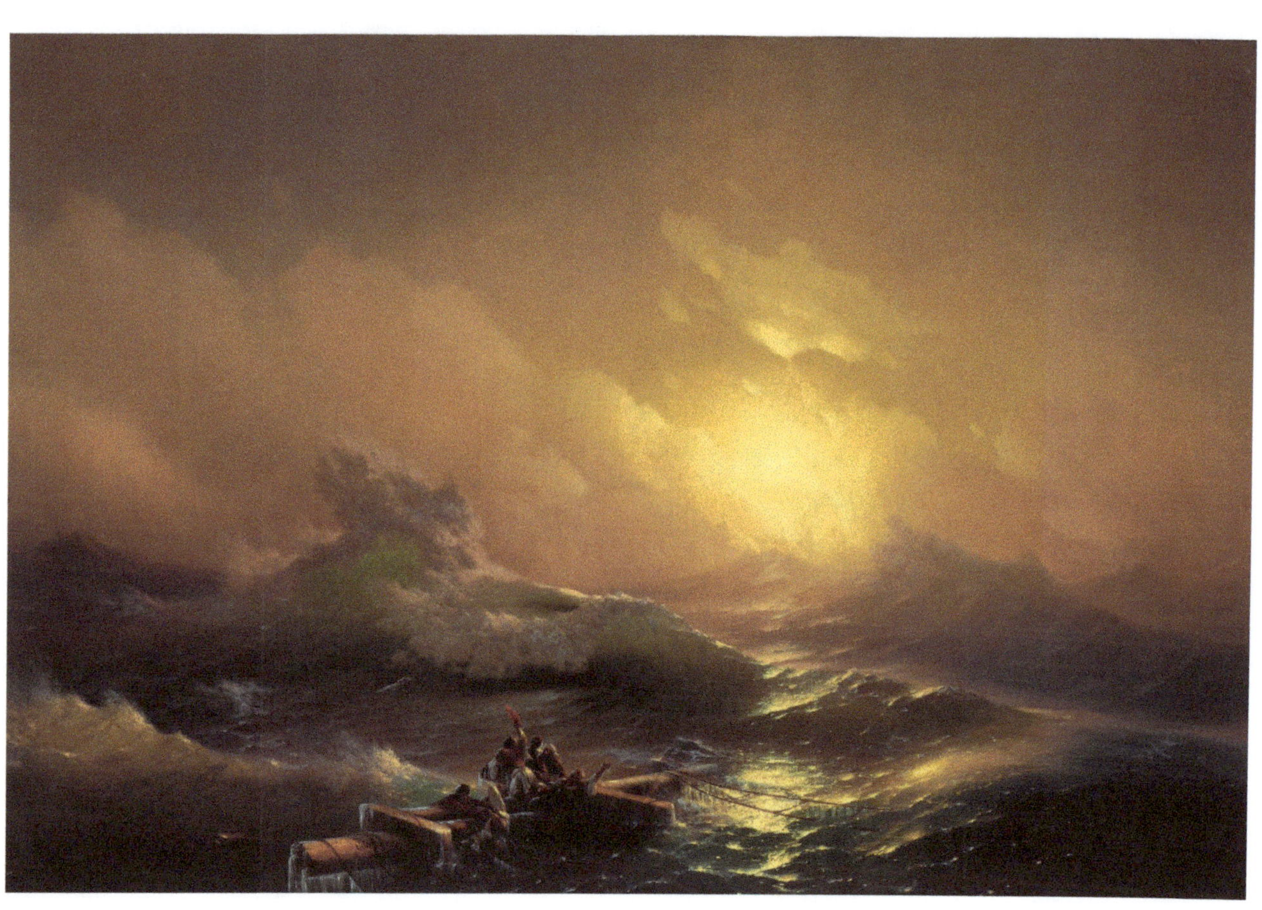

reversal of the situation and put him back in favour with the orthodox point of view.

He was seen as the saviour who was needed: the idiosyncratic features of his genius were ignored whilst his science and energy were put at the forefront. In 1825 he was elected a member of the *Institut.*

In 1825 Charles X was crowned in Reims. Gothic decoration was chosen for the ceremony: there was a gallery in front of the façade as well as inside the nave. These solemn circumstances helped assert the triumph of the Middle Ages that had been so looked down on. Everything worked in favour of this reversal: it was in the interest of religion and politics whilst being also supported by the development of historic sciences. In 1831 the novel *Notre-Dame* de Paris made the craze for medievalism reach its peak. It was visible everywhere, in the inspiration of artists and writers, trinkets, furniture and fashion.

David's death in Brussels at the beginning of 1826 went almost unnoticed. A few weeks later an exhibition of Greek art was held. Some of the School's most famous paintings were displayed, besides which Delacroix, Devéria, Roqueplan and Scheffer also exhibited their work. The stylistic confrontation had exactly the effect that could have been expected: faded enthusiasms were revived and avant-garde artists were crushed by the weight of the glorious past. However, all was in vain

◀ **Ivan Aivazovsky,**
The Ninth Wave, 1850.
Oil on canvas, 221 x 332 cm.
The State Russian Museum, St Petersburg.

and the dying body could not be brought back to life. Nevertheless, the Romantics lost some support, and from then on they were attacked mercilessly.

1827 was marked by the preface to *Cromwell.* The parallel between Hugo and Delacroix, which was to become famous, was first made by Louis Vitet in the Globe. The artistic struggle reached its peak, and the Exhibition of 1827 turned into a 'convention on painting',as a contemporary put it. Delacroix's *Sardanapale,* Devéria's *Birth of Henri IV,* and Ary Scheffer's *Souliot Women* were to be seen. Opposite that group there were *The Death of Elisabeth* and *The Taking of the Trocadero* by Paul Delaroche, *Mazeppa* by Horace Vernet, and *Torquato Tasso* by Robert Fleury. Bonington displayed *The View of Venice* and Lawrence *Master Lambton.* Such a list gives testimony to an exceptional creative intensity. Inspired, feverish, solid or skilful; how could those paintings not trouble minds? Sigalon failed totally. So did Delacroix, whose *Marin Faliero* did not raise any interest whilst *Sardanapale* was slated equally by his friends and enemies. It was a success for Boulanger and a short-lived triumph for the creator of *The Birth of Henri IV,* Eugène Devéria, of whom it was briefly thought that he might become the leader of the Romantics. Two beginners, Corot and Paul Huet, were hardly noticed in the turmoil yet it was through them that landscapes would be included in the controversy.

A few days after the Exhibition started some new rooms opened at the Louvre. On one of the ceilings Ingres had painted *The Apotheosis of Homer.* To tell the truth, no-one understood it, and it prompted mostly the admiration of the Romantics.

The first performance of the play *Henri III and his Court* by Alexandre Dumas on 10 February 1829 was not solely a literary event. It revealed some deep changes in the performing arts. Doric porticos which could hardly fill the stage were no longer fashionable; staging, décor and costumes grew richer and were enlivened by Romantic inspiration.

The opening of the Conservatoire's concerts by Habeneck in 1828 allowed music lovers to discover and develop the cult of Beethoven. Around the end of 1830, Berlioz conducted his *Symphonie fantastique*. He transferred into the realm of music the same enthusiasm and rage that was going on in painting and poetry, and thus found himself, like Victor Hugo or Delacroix, a key figure in the *avant-garde*.

The revolution had just begun. It created generous exaltation and a lot of hope. It seemed that the France which had been humiliated under the Restoration regime was about to be reborn. *Freedom guiding the People* by Delacroix was the sign of that élan. Had it endured, the direction taken by the arts would have been substantially different. Reconciled with their time and bathed in civic spirit, artists would have forgotten their reveries and feverish feelings and would have been reconnected to reality. *The Monarchie de Juillet*, dispelled illusions born on the barricades almost immediately. Artists turned back to the silence of their studios.

Yet the new regime provided fighters in unexpected fields of activity. Political caricature sprang up with an incredible violence and fierceness but also unbelievable artistic brilliance. Decamps, Raffet and Grandville opened the way to Daumier, and when

the laws of September 1834 stopped their sarcasm against Louis-Philippe their satirical wittiness started targeting public mores, and Gavarni applied his sharp mind with endless resourcefulness.

Around that time David's school seemed utterly exhausted. Gros's suicide, after the bad reception of his works at the 1835 Exhibition had driven him to despair, could be perceived as a token gesture. Of course that did not prevent followers of David from going on with their teaching, keeping their seats at the *Institut*, and providing an increased number of bloodless, conventional and outrageous paintings to decorate the monuments and churches of Paris in particular. The Institut, that had the juries of exhibitions under its control, proscribed people like Delacroix, Decamps, Chassériau and, above all, landscape painters throughout the Monarchie de Juillet.

Delacroix was fully accomplished by then. He painted the admirable *Algiers Women* in 1834, *Saint Sebastian* in 1836, *Medea* and *Taillebourg* in 1838, *Trajan* and *The Shipwreck of Don* uan in 1840, The *Crusaders of Constantinople* in 1841 and *Marcus Aurelius* in 1845. Decamps created high quality works with the same regularity. Chassériau, a child prodigy brought up in Ingres's studio, asked the Romantics to help him express his refined and complex desires. In his famous lessons on colour, Chevreul justified Delacroix's technical intuitions

Francisco de Goya y Lucientes, ▶
The Third of May, 1808:
The Execution of the Defenders of Madrid, 1814.
Oil on canvas, 268 x 347 cm.
Museo Nacional del Prado, Madrid.

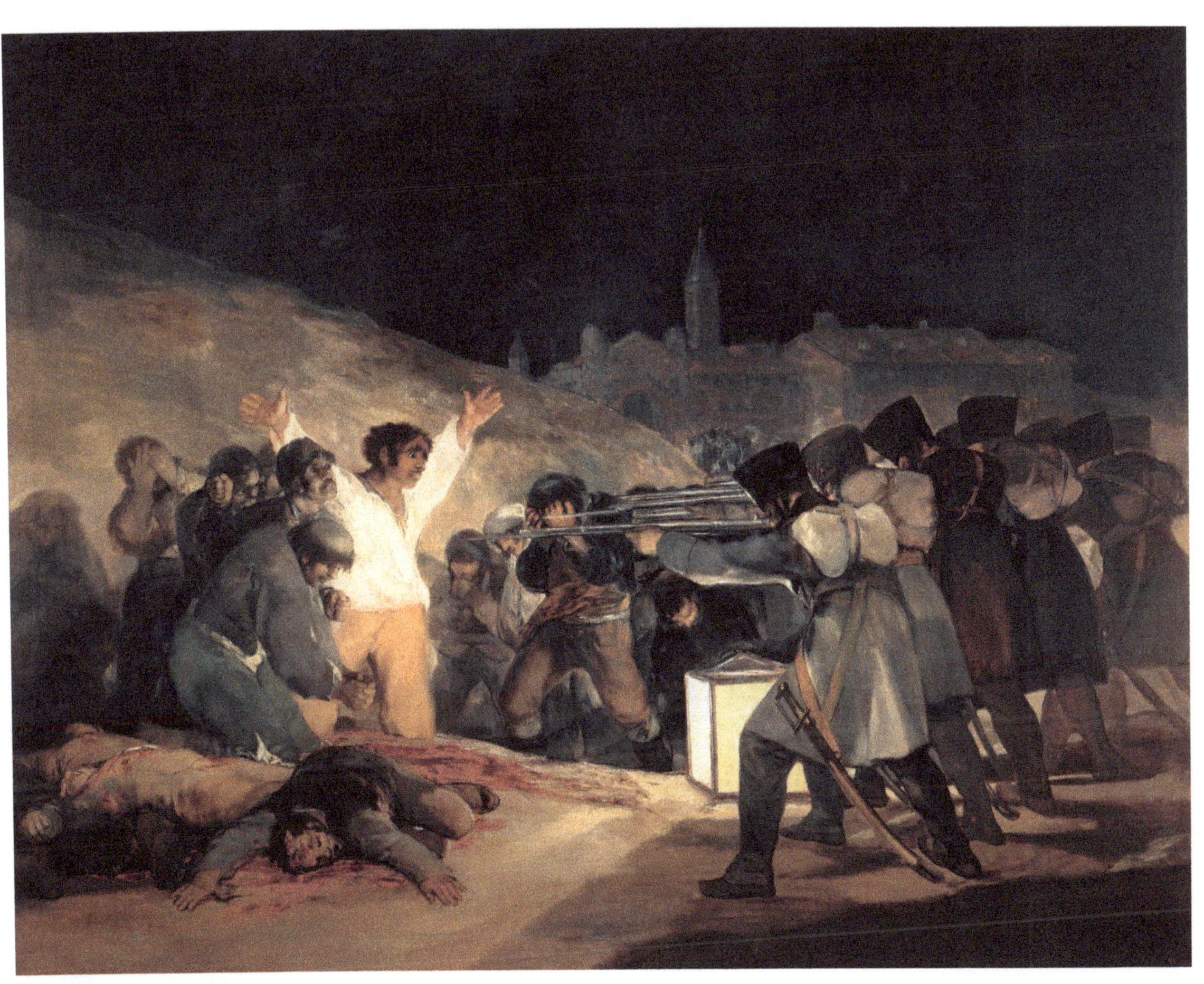

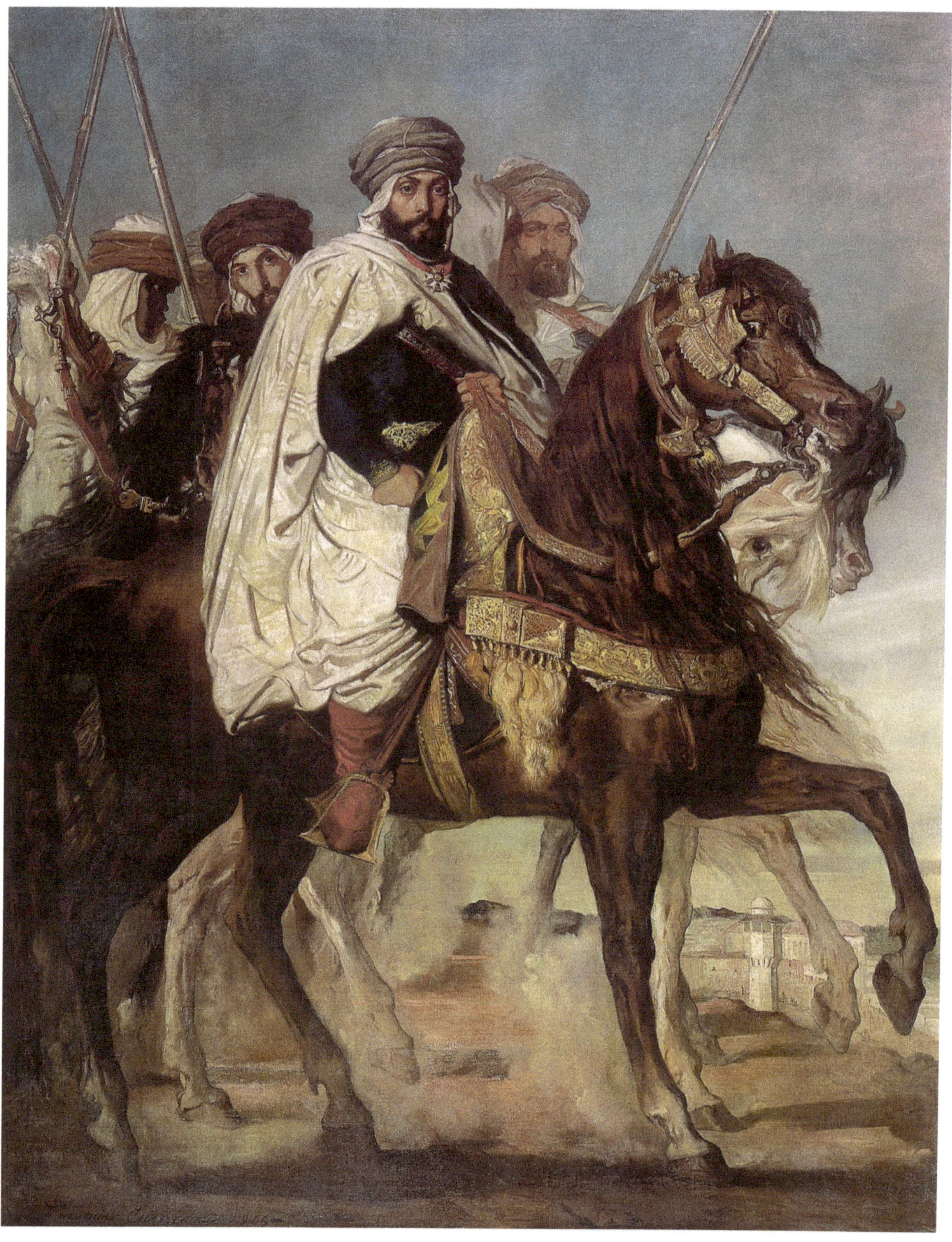

and drew up new laws that could allow daring ideas to develop.

Revolution had expanded everywhere. Landscape painting was bubbling with excitement. An imposing group made up of Paul Huet, Dupré, Théodore Rousseau, Daubigny and Corot offered original ways of feeling and representing natural landscapes. At the Exhibition of 1827, *Mercury* by Rude foreshadowed a renewal in sculpture stamped with authority. Turmoil reached sculpture too. David d'Angers modelled statues, busts and medallions of his most famous contemporaries and sculpted the pediment of the Panthéon in 1837. On the Arc de Triomphe, Rude celebrated *the Departure* of the revolutionary armies with epic grandeur and Barye managed to catch and represent the lively ferocity of the great cats.

Parallel to that, a craze for images developed and lithography played a central role. Illustrations started to appear everywhere in books. Whilst the monumental publication of the *Voyages pittoresques et romantiques dans l'ancienne France* was going on, enriched by lithographs, some of the most beautiful of which were carried out by Bonington and Isabey, books of all kinds were adorned with frontispieces, images, lithographs, etchings and steel engravings. With the help of incredibly skilful craftsmen, wood allowed illustrations of perfect typographic

◀ **Théodore Chassériau**,
Ali Ben Ahmed, the Last Caliph of Constantine,
with his Entourage outside Constantine, 1845.
Oil on canvas, 325 x 260 cm.
Musée national du château et des Trianons, Versailles.

quality to be inserted in the text. The *Magasin pittoresque* relied heavily on images in its effort at encyclopaedic popularisation.

Deep changes were also visible in furniture, interior design, clothing and even hairdressing: tasteful or not, art was taken into consideration in all areas. Collectors gathered marvels from the past and threw new light upon them. The choice of a jacket or haircut or the growth of a beard showed aesthetic beliefs and were perceived as manifestos. Without knowing it, elegant men and ladies going to the opera disguised as transvestites, slovenly-dressed young people complaining about the fuss ordered by Chicard, all took up the style established by the Duchess of Berry and Alexandre Dumas. Unexpected costumes, unreliable archaeological extravaganzas, plastic surprises, medleys of colour and flashiness, all were a visual feast added to music or dance.

Was the whole movement a hundred per cent Romantic? Undoubtedly analysis reveals that some aspects were not a matter for Romanticism but parodies, imitations and compromises would not have happened if some active and vivid ferment had not been at work, modelling the period, and people of the time, whether scandalised or overjoyed, saw Romanticism everywhere.

Indeed, Romanticism had swept across the whole of society. Yet, at the same time that one could see signs of it everywhere, it was already deeply eroded and going into decline. Just after the first battles, Romanticism faced some opposition in the public which it was not going to overcome. I am not referring here to the surprise that Romantic works caused, for every new form of art requires some time for the public to adapt, become educated and eventually understand it. It is also obvious that the eccentric side of early Romanticism would only raise momentary curiosity. No, the essence of Romanticism itself was repugnant to the spirit in general, and the French spirit in particular.

With traditions of clarity, order, logic and analysis and the pre-eminence of rational thinking, everything in France was against an aesthetic movement which praised feeling and passion and relied on the soul's intimate forces instead of asking for well thought out adhesion.

Romantic success was never total and the more characteristic the works, the more the polemic reactions they caused. Year after year the general atmosphere was less and less in the Romantics' favour. Besides, material wealth softened the *mal du siècle*. When time came for minds to be taken over by new passions, social and humanitarian tendencies as well as political claims called for action, and focused everybody's attention on the realities of the time, preparing for new artistic ideals.

The defection of artists themselves was a serious sign of the movement running out of steam. Louis Boulanger, for whom Hugo cherished great hopes and whose zeal had led him to truly extravagant behaviour, finally turned to dull and spineless painting. Overwhelmed by the weight of early glory, and despite a few successful comebacks, Eugène Devéria disappeared too. Ary Scheffer turned his back on the colourfulness of *Gaston of Foix* and preferred pale philosophical abstraction.

Others looked only for success and, in order to achieve it, they weakened their effects, added mannerism and, in the end, produced watered-down Romanticism. Some tried to revive the graces of the eighteenth century that they had talked down in the past. Achille Devéria and Célestin Nanteuil came down with a bump and produced undemanding lithographs.

The crowd seemed to prefer skilful men who produced mundane or dramatic images using a plain language devoid of technical originality. Avatars, weaknesses of disoriented artists and an uneducated public all had a negative impact but then an even more damaging phenomenon occurred. From 1840 on, the suppressed classical tendencies found a new vigour and claimed revenge; public opinion called for a reaction and young people turned away from Romanticism. Victor Hugo's play *The Burgraves* was a memorable failure, and Ingres suddenly appeared like the hero of the hour. He was just back from Italy, where he had managed the *Ecole de Rome* and had had an incredible influence on his pupils. He had just painted the *Stratonice*, which was showered with praise. He was acclaimed as a saviour and humbly agreed to stand up in the sacred cause of art. He had soon forgotten his previous ambitions and with total authority he proclaimed the cult of the beautiful and condemned any deviation from the rule. He had only a few direct disciples but, nevertheless, dull and faded paintings reappeared everywhere. Neo-classical landscape painters turned

Eugène Delacroix, ▶
The Massacre at Chios, 1824.
Oil on canvas, 419 x 354 cm.
Musée du Louvre, Paris.

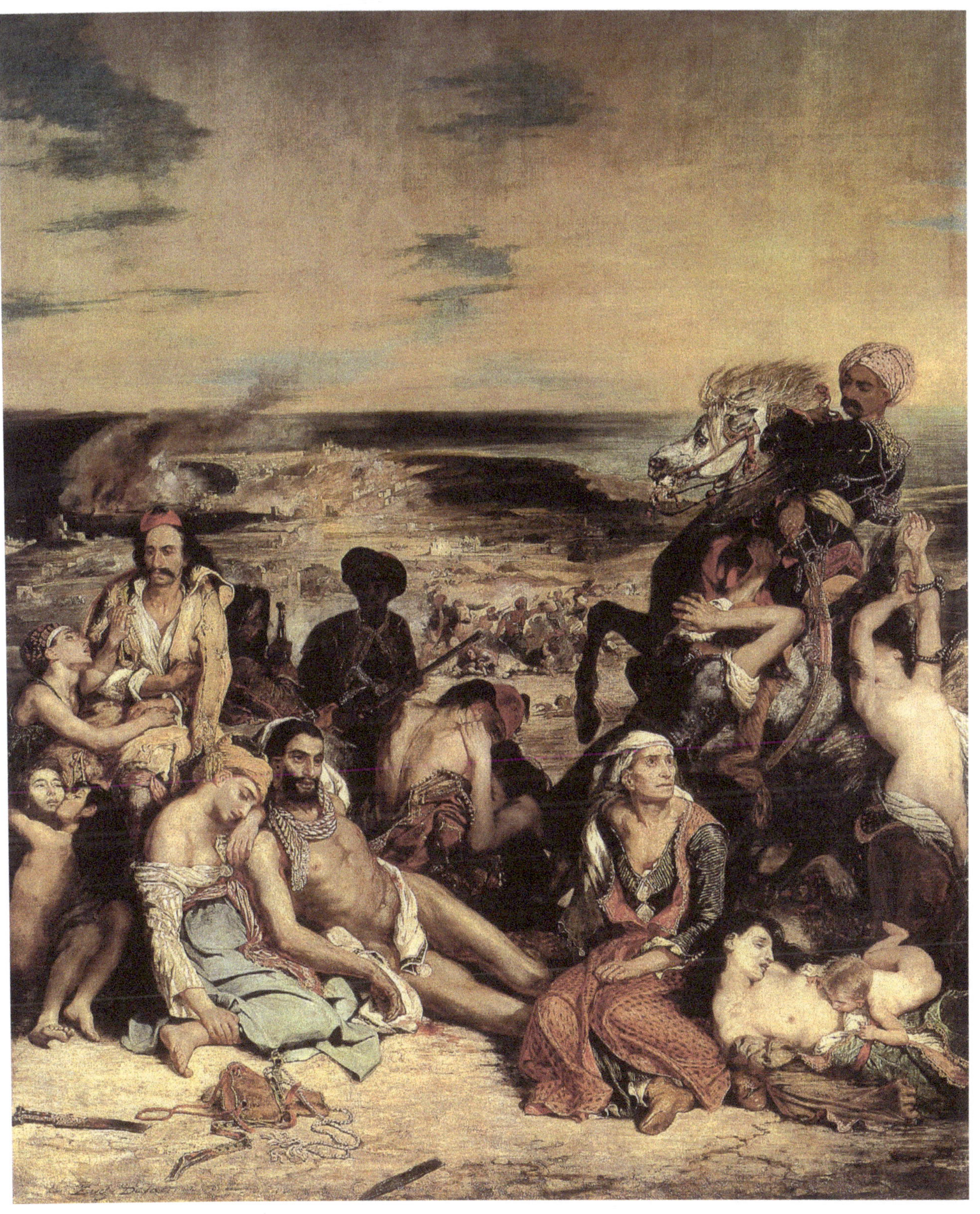

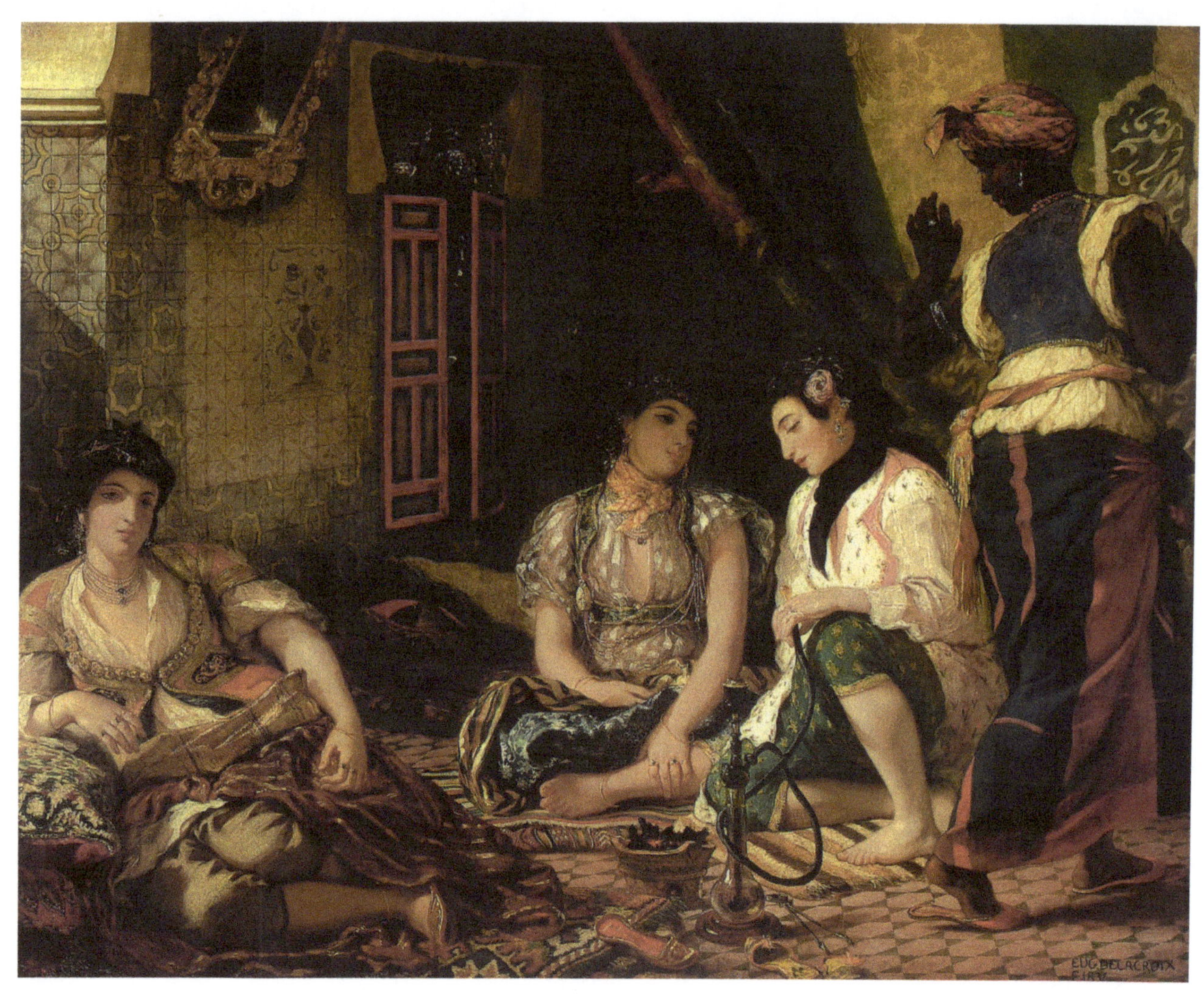

▲ **Eugène Delacroix,**
The Women of Algiers, 1834.
Oil on canvas, 180 x 229 cm.
Musée du Louvre, Paris.

to Antiquity again and were influenced by Poussin. The general appearance of exhibitions changed completely: colour, movement and life disappeared. Romantic art was still allowed in, but seemed out of place. Greyness and a sense of wisdom had swept in. An English man felt like going for a cold bath as he entered the Exhibition of 1846. New artists appeared like Gérôme with his *Cockfighting*; the calculated and glamorous effects of the *Decadent Romans* by Couture appeared vivid and inspired.

It was a time of helplessness. Hyperbolic assertions, polemic beliefs and basic negation were not worthwhile anymore. Either out of scepticism or indifference the most sensitive people accepted the novelties that stood out, whatever doctrine they stemmed from. They preached eclecticism, and events seemed to prove them right. Times were weary though each year probably had its harvest of works worth admiring. Some were as good or even possibly superior to the works of the previous years but their flaws and qualities were precisely the same that had been debated *ad nauseam*. A feeling of general discomfort and stagnation gradually developed, awaiting the advent of the man, the idea or the work that would be capable of reviving energies, enthusing a new spirit and stirring up art out of its dullness. At that time precisely a whole chain of events occurred, the importance of which people of the time could not realise. They appear to us, however, as the portents of a new faith, the revelation of which was awaited. On several occasions, works containing elements of poetry focused on reality praised by Géricault were exhibited. Since *The Readers* in 1840, Meissonier had accustomed the public to meticulous accuracy.

The opening of a Spanish gallery at the Louvre in 1848 showed the example of masters filled with an intense naturalist feeling. The daguerreotype was invented in 1839 and photography focused everybody's attention on views of direct reality once again. At the same time, Balzac, Stendhal and George Sand analysed contemporary life.

Thus realism crept into art and society through obscure and complex mechanisms. At first it only seemed to be claiming a small place but soon it asserted itself as the only truth and that it was up to the realist to regenerate the arts. At the last Exhibitions of the Monarchie de Juillet, two young painters had a modest start as no-one, not even themselves, guessed their potential. Then came the 1848 Revolution and Courbet and Millet discovered their own genius in the middle of the universal turmoil. Amidst a blaze of publicity they proclaimed the beliefs that were at the core of artistic battles. Of course some artists whose soul was definitely Romantic were going to remain: neither Delacroix nor Berlioz or Préault would give up their ideals and they could neither be forgotten nor despised. They would remain a reference for young people and, in a way, would continue to have more influence than ever. However, the continuing action of Romanticism would be of a different kind now, somewhat pacified and somewhat historical. In 1848 a new period started for the arts; Romantic times were over.

▼ **Joseph Mallord William Turner,**
The Burning of the Houses of Lords and Commons, October 16, 1834, c. 1834-1835.
Oil on canvas, 92.1 x 123.2 cm.
Philadelphia Museum of Art, Philadelphia.

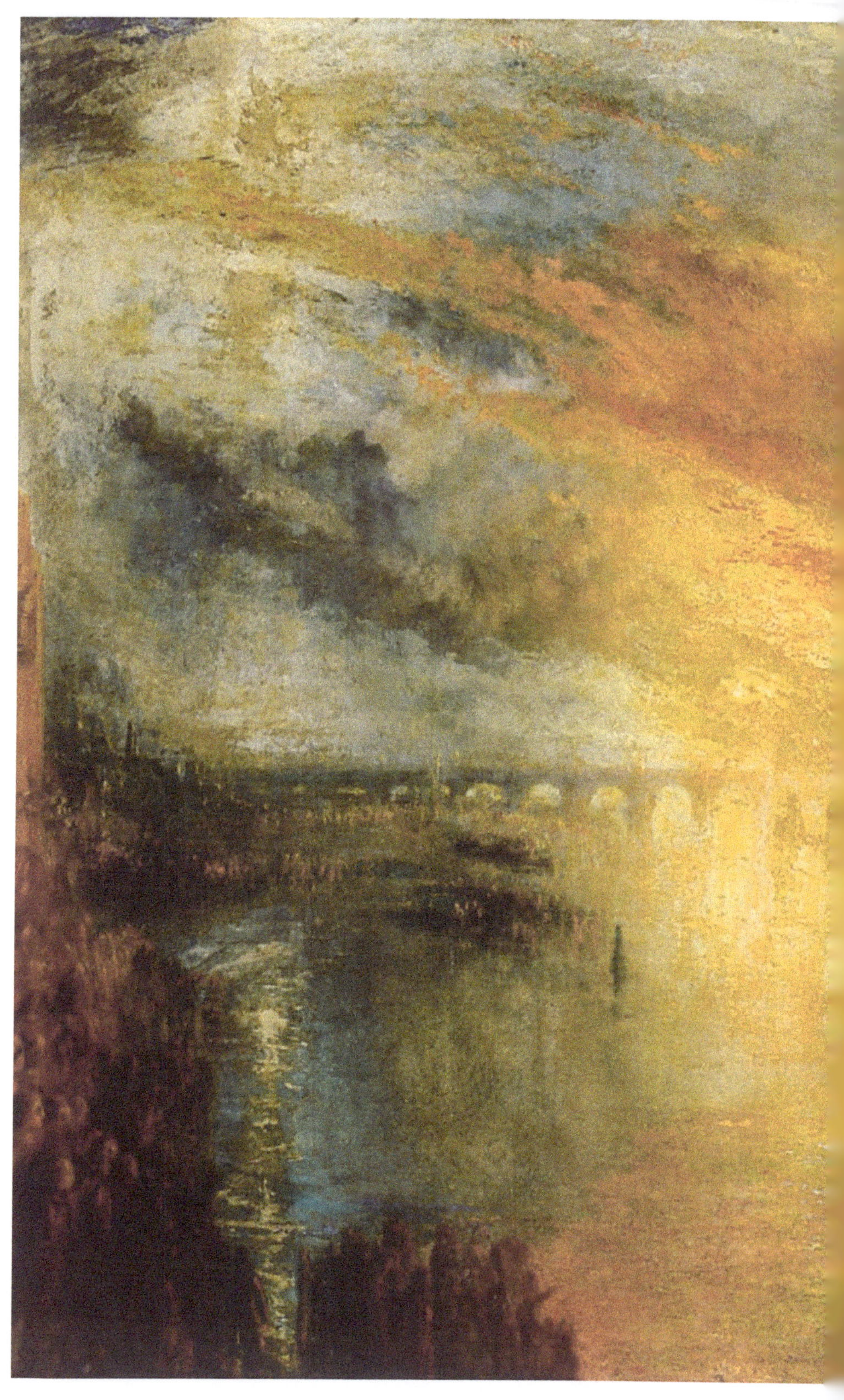

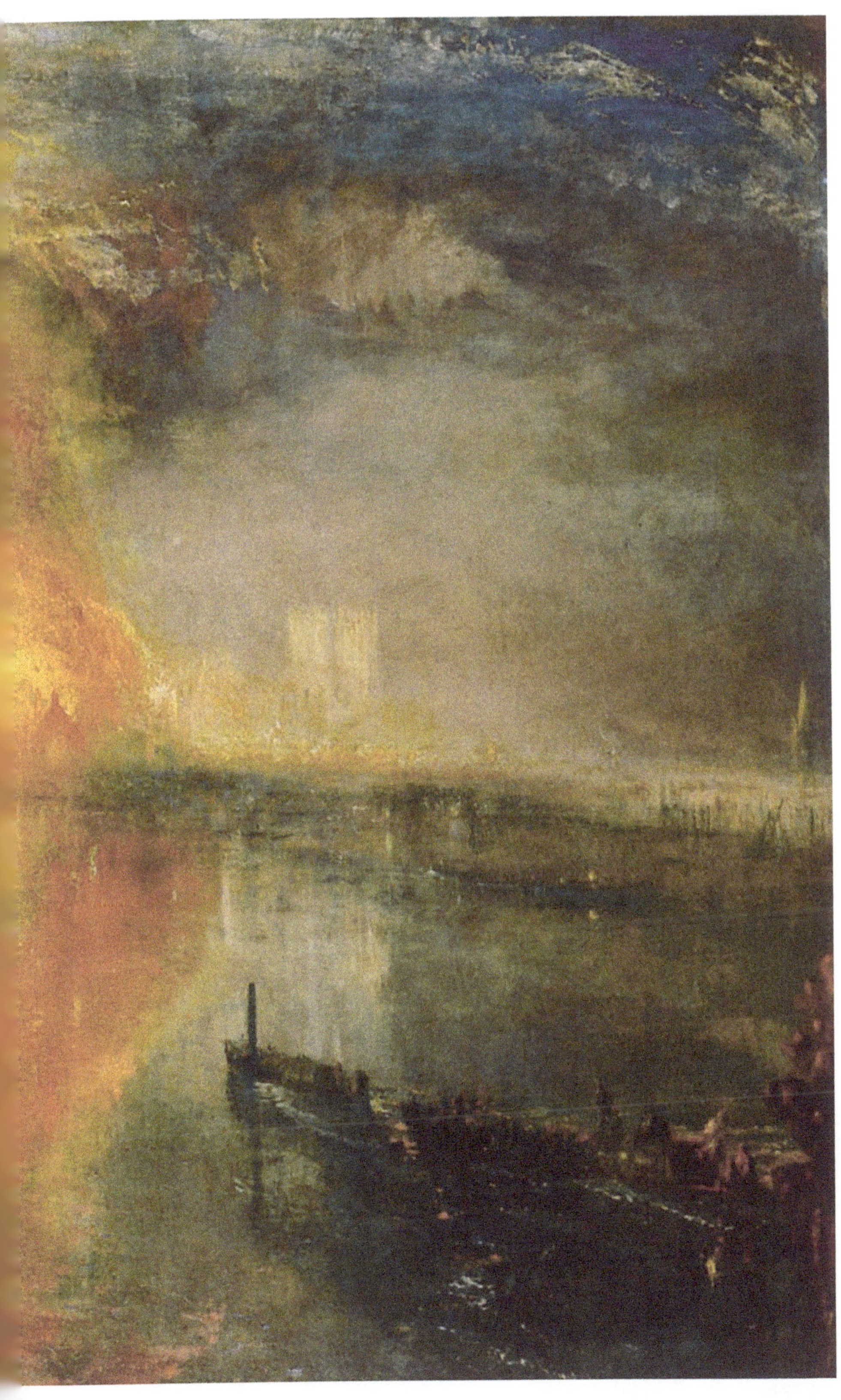

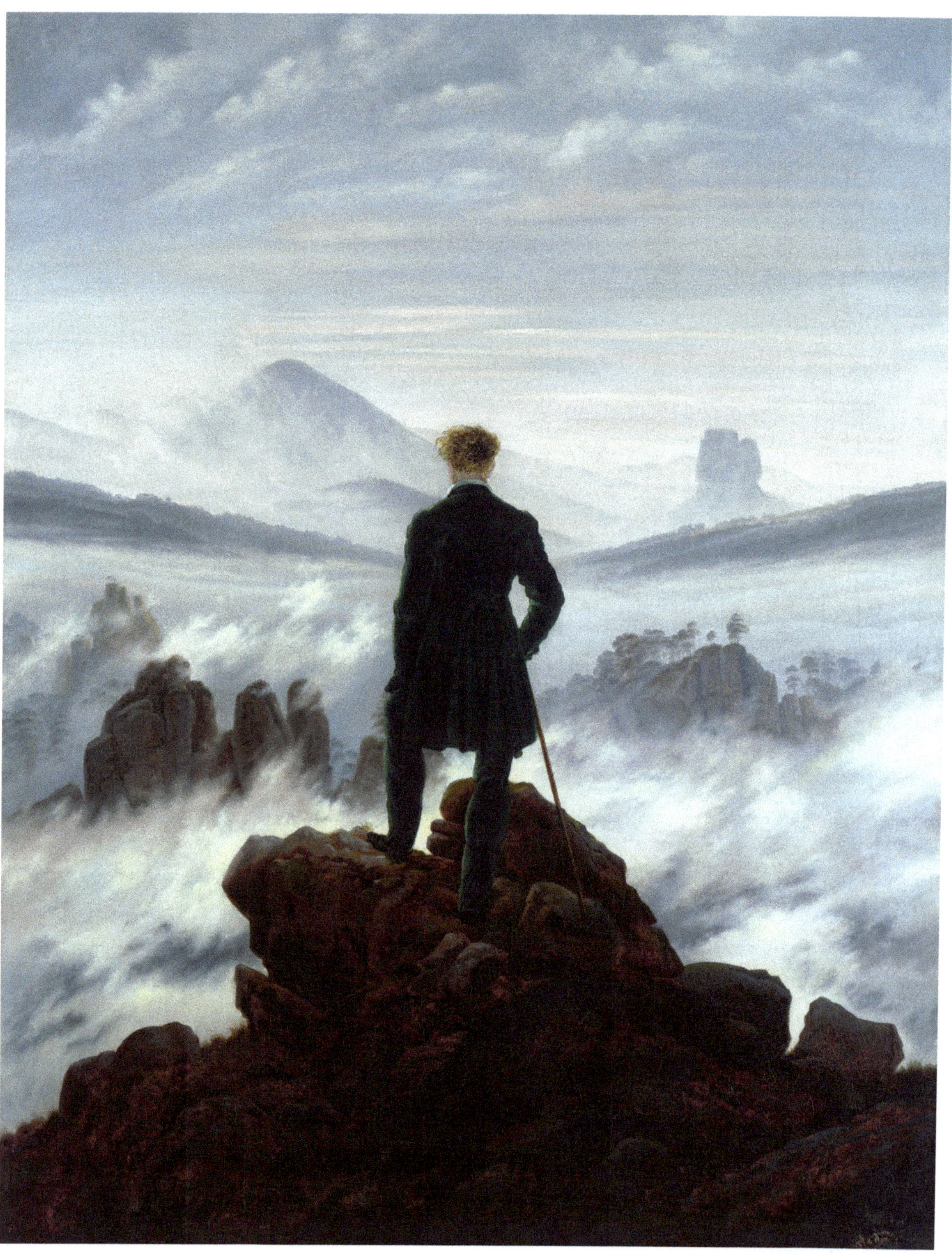

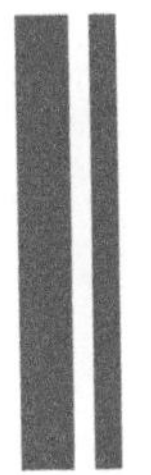

MAJOR ARTISTS

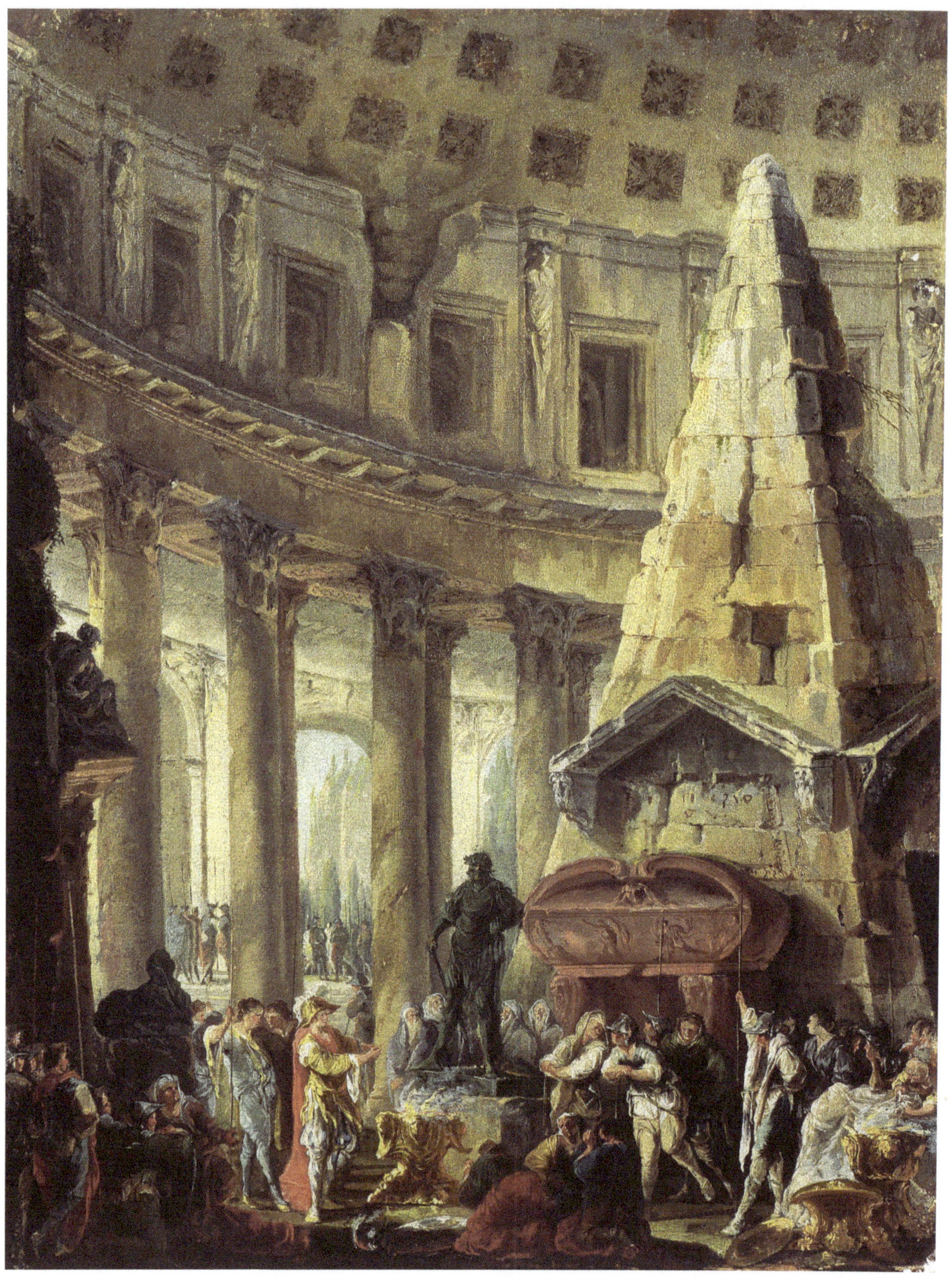

HUBERT ROBERT

(Paris, 1733-1808)

Hubert Robert was the son of a Nicolas Robert, who worked in the Marquis of Choiseul Stainville's household, a connection that was helpful to Hubert throughout his life. From 1751 to 1754 he studied under the French sculptor Michel-Ange Slodtz, who in fact encouraged him to paint. He then left for Rome at the age of twenty-one, where he stayed for eleven years, at first joining the French Academy. There he spent time with Piranesi's circle, taking much influence from the Italian artist's etchings of Rome, and executed many outdoor sketches of ruins and Roman buildings. The contrast between the ruins of ancient Rome and his own time excited his keenest interest and, although he had started for Italy independently, the credit he there acquired procured him the protection of the minister Marigny and an official allowance. During this time he became acquainted with the Abbé de Saint-Non, who would later produce many engravings of his work, and who took Robert and the artist Jean-Honoré Fragonard on a trip to Naples and Pompeii.

In 1765 Robert returned to Paris to meet with great success. He first exhibited his work in the Salon of 1767, and it was extremely well received.

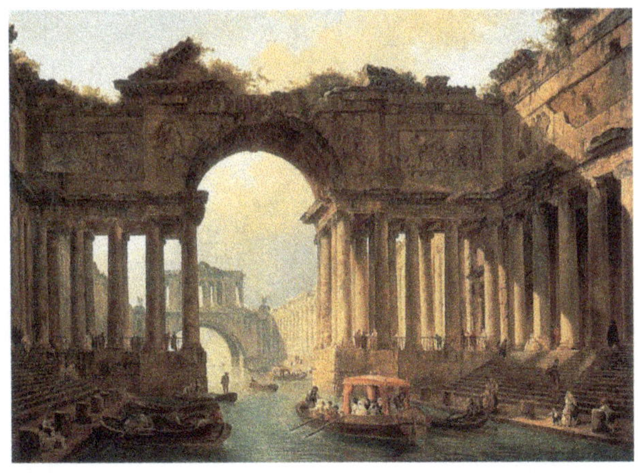

▲ **Hubert Robert**,
Landscape with Architecture and a Canal, 1783.
Oil on canvas, 129 x 182.5 cm.
The State Hermitage Museum, St Petersburg.

▲ **Caspar David Friedrich**,
The Wanderer above the Mists, c. 1817-1818.
Oil on canvas, 94.8 x 74.8 cm.
Hamburger Kunsthalle, Hamburg.

◄ **Hubert Robert**,
Alexander the Great Visiting the Tomb of Achilles, 1755-1760.
Oil on canvas, 63 x 48 cm.
Private collection.

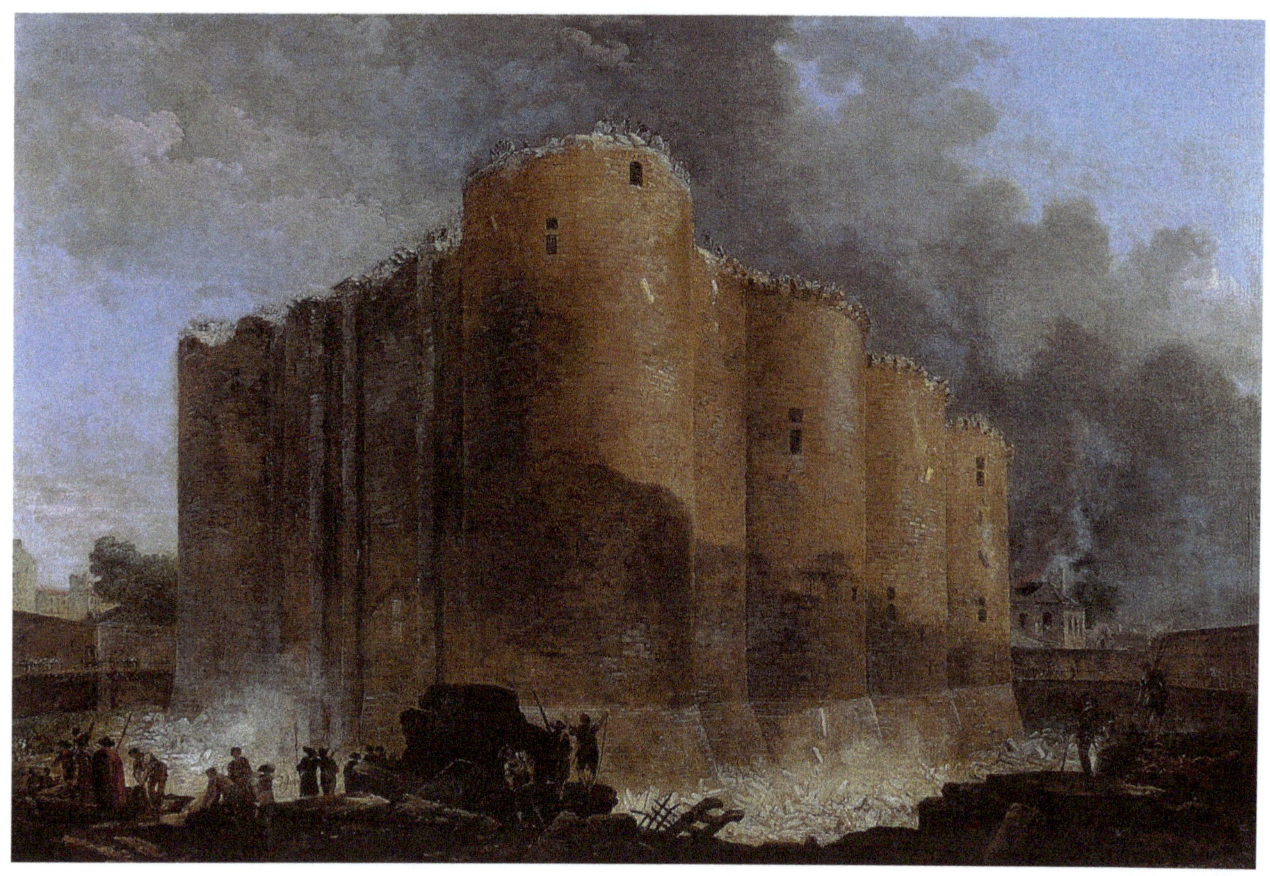

He became known as "Robert-les-ruines" for his depictions of romantically-lit ruins set in idealised surroundings, some of which were imaginary, such as his *View of the Great Gallery in the Louvre in Ruins* (1796), but many of which were based on direct observational sketches. His incessant activity as an artist, his daring character and his many adventures attracted general sympathy and admiration. In the fourth canto of his *L'Imagination*, Jacques Delille celebrated Robert's miraculous escape when lost in the Catacombs; later in life, when imprisoned during the Terror and marked for the guillotine, through a fatal accident another died in his place and Robert lived. Robert eventually died of apoplexy on the 15th April 1808.

This French artist deserves to be remembered not so much for his skill as a painter as for the liveliness and focus with which he treated the subjects he painted. The quantity of his work is immense: the Louvre alone contains over two hundred works by his hand and specimens are frequently to be met with in provincial museums and private collections. Robert's work has a scenic quality that brought about his selection by Voltaire to paint the decorations of his theatre at Ferney. In Italy his work was frequently reproduced by Liénard amongst others.

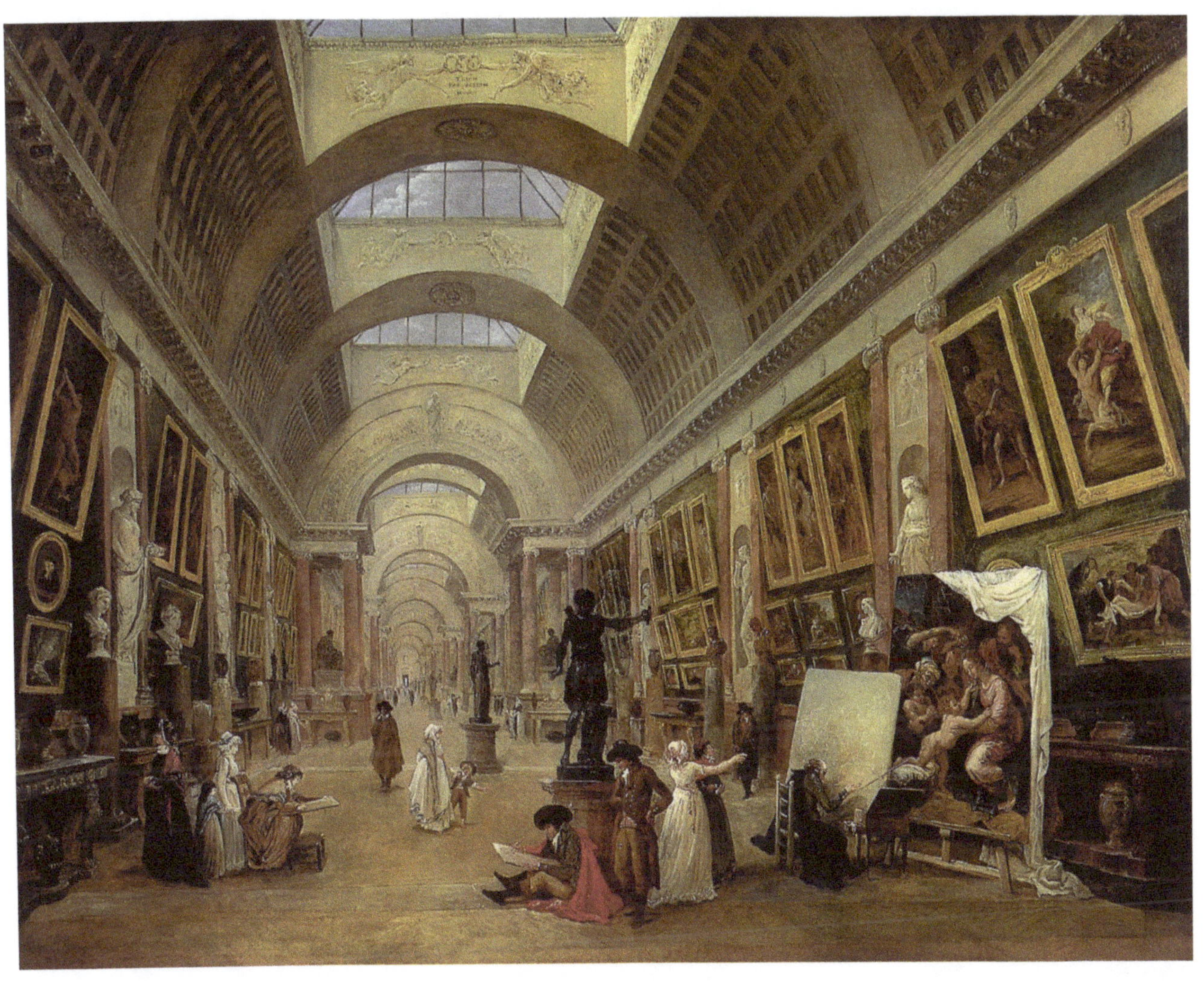

◄ **Hubert Robert**,
Demolition of the Bastille, 1789.
Oil on canvas, 77 x 114 cm.
Musée Carnavalet – musée d'Histoire de Paris, Paris.

▲ **Hubert Robert**,
Design for the Grande Galerie in the Louvre, 1796.
Oil on canvas, 115 x 145 cm.
Musée du Louvre, Paris.

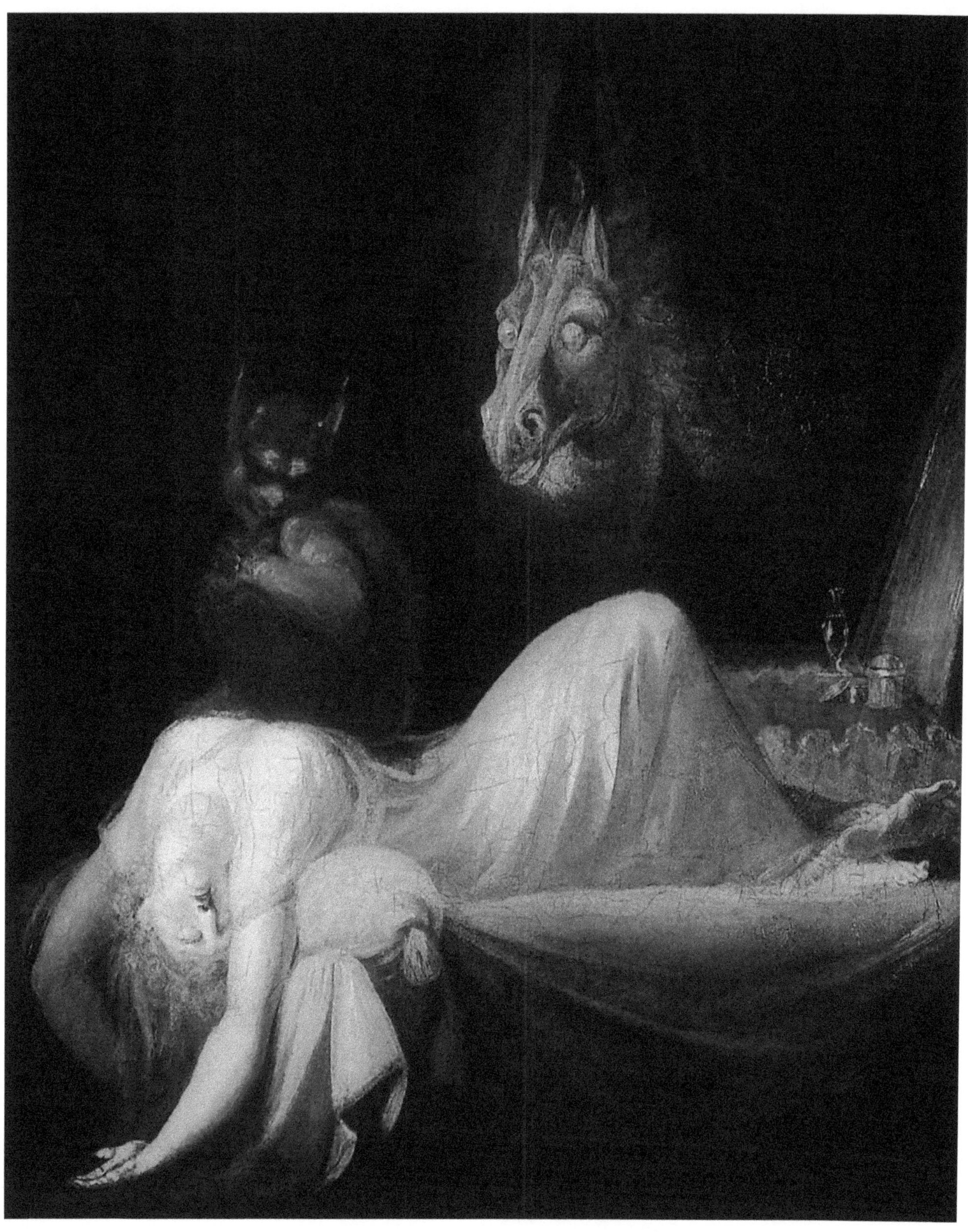

JOHANN HEINRICH FÜSSLI, CALLED HENRY FUSELI

(Zürich 1741 – London 1825)

An English painter and writer on art, of German-Swiss family, Fuseli was born in Zürich in Switzerland on the 7th February 1741. His father was John Caspar Füssli, a painter. Fuseli's father intended him for the church, and with this view sent him to the Caroline college of his native town, where he received an excellent classical education.

After taking orders in 1761 Fuseli was obliged to leave his country in consequence of having aided the exposure of an unjust magistrate, whose family was still powerful enough to make its vengeance felt. He first travelled through Germany and then, in 1765, visited England, where he supported himself for some time with writing. He became acquainted with Sir Joshua Reynolds, to whom he showed his drawings. On Sir Joshua's advice he then devoted himself wholly to art. In 1770 he made an artistic pilgrimage to Italy, where he remained till 1778, changing his name from Füssli to Fuseli, as it sounded more Italian. Early in 1779 he returned to England via Zürich. He found a commission awaiting him from an Alderman Boydell, who was then organising his celebrated Shakespeare gallery. Fuseli painted a number of pieces for this patron.

As a painter, Fuseli was inventive and original and ever aspiring to the highest forms of excellence. His mind was capable of grasping and realising the loftiest conceptions, which, however, he often spoilt on the canvas by exaggerating the proportions, and throwing his figures into attitudes of fantastic and over-strained contortion. He delighted in the supernatural and Idealised his compositions, believing a certain amount of exaggeration necessary in historical painting. "Damn Nature! She always puts me out," was his characteristic exclamation. In this theory he was confirmed by the study of Michelangelo's works and the marble statues of the Monte Cavallo. But this idea was carried out to excess by him. A striking illustration of this occurs in his picture of *Hamlet and the Ghost*: Hamlet, it has been said, looks as if he would burst his clothes with convulsive cramps in his muscles.

On the other hand, his paintings are never languid or cold. His figures are full of life, earnestness and

◀ **Henry Fuseli,**
The Nightmare, 1790-1791.
Oil on canvas, 76 x 63 cm.
Goethe-Museum, Frankfurt am Main.

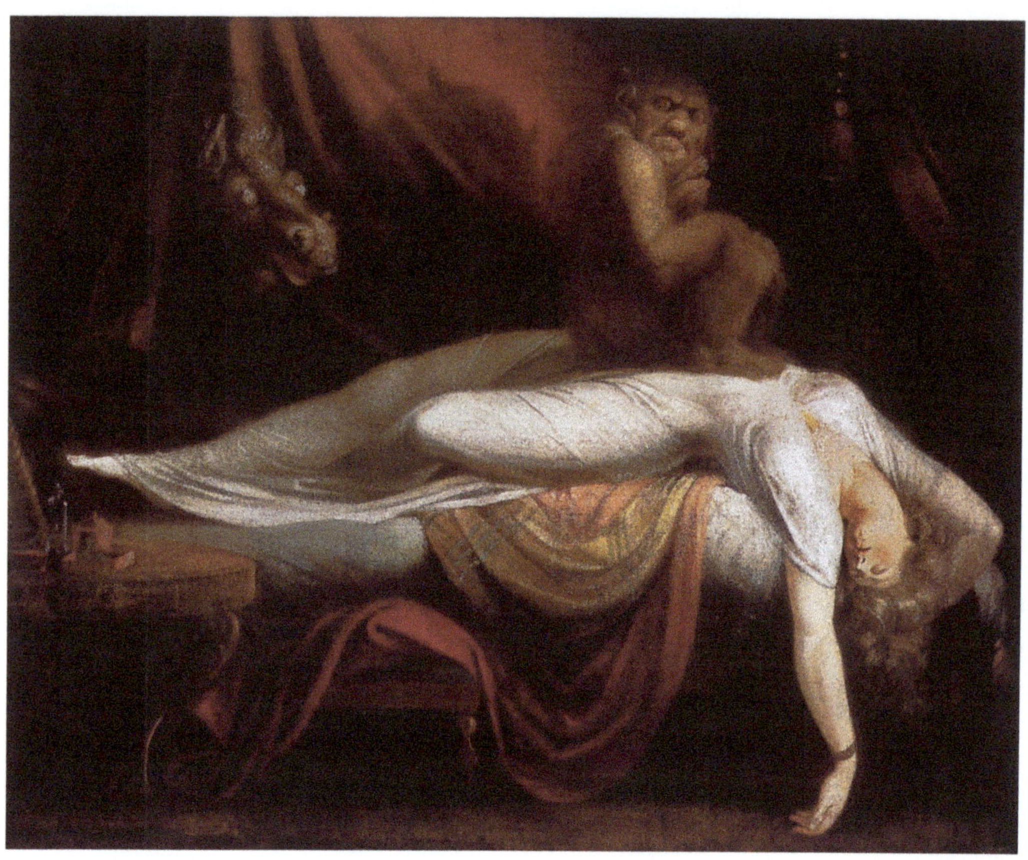

intense purpose. Like Rubens he excelled in the art of setting his figures in motion. Though the lofty and terrible was his proper sphere, Fuseli had fine perception of the ludicrous. The grotesque humour of his fairy scenes, especially those from A Midsummer Night's Dream, is in its way not less remarkable than the poetic power of his more ambitious works. As a colourist Fuseli has but small claims to distinction. He scorned to set a palette as most artists do; he merely dashed his tints recklessly over it. This recklessness may perhaps be explained by the fact that he did not paint in oil until he was twenty-five years of age. Despite these drawbacks he possessed the elements of a great painter.

Fuseli painted more than two hundred pictures, but he exhibited only a minority of them. His first painting to excite particular attention was the *Nightmare*, exhibited in 1782. His sketches or designs number about eight hundred; they have admirable qualities of invention and design, and are frequently superior to his paintings.

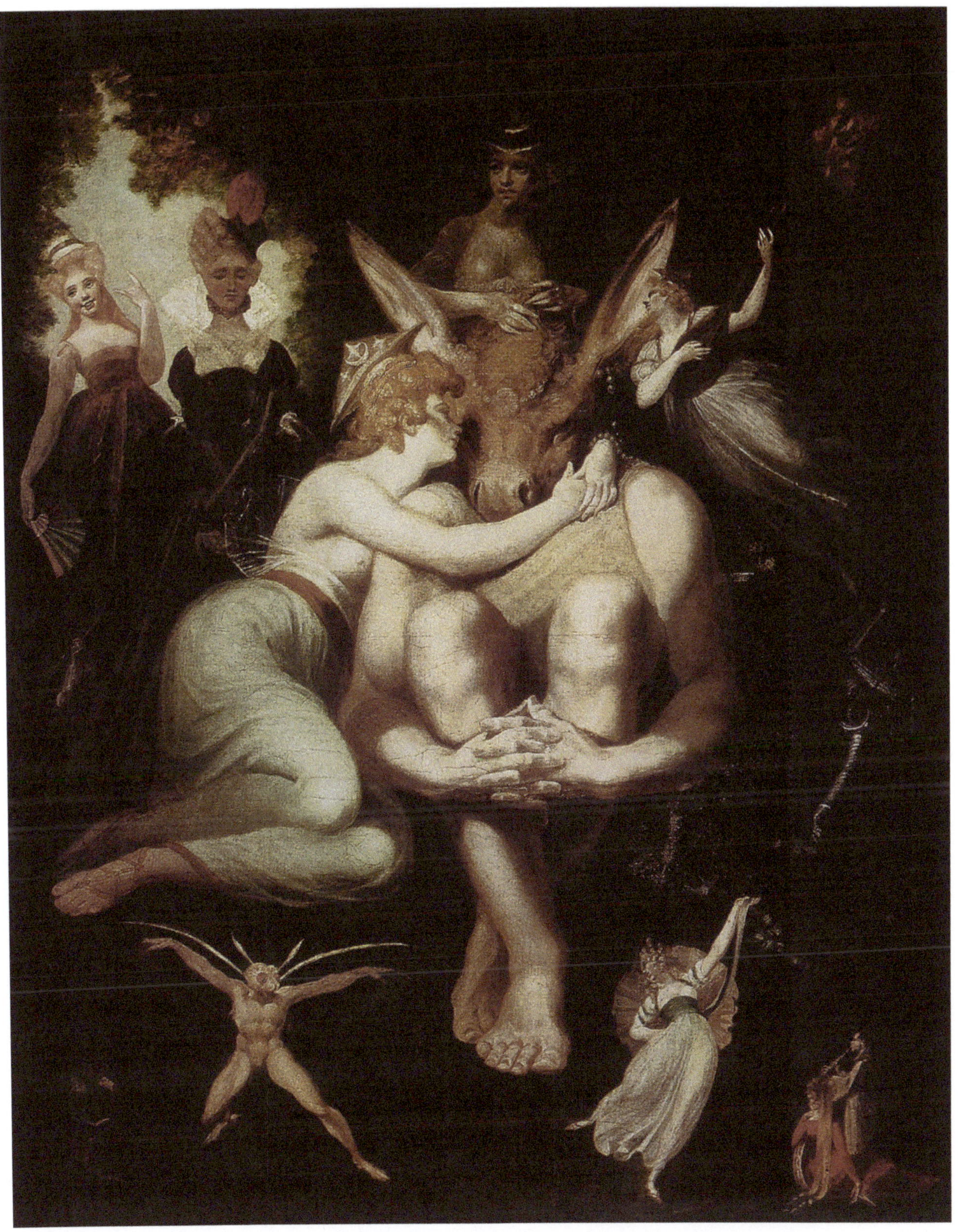

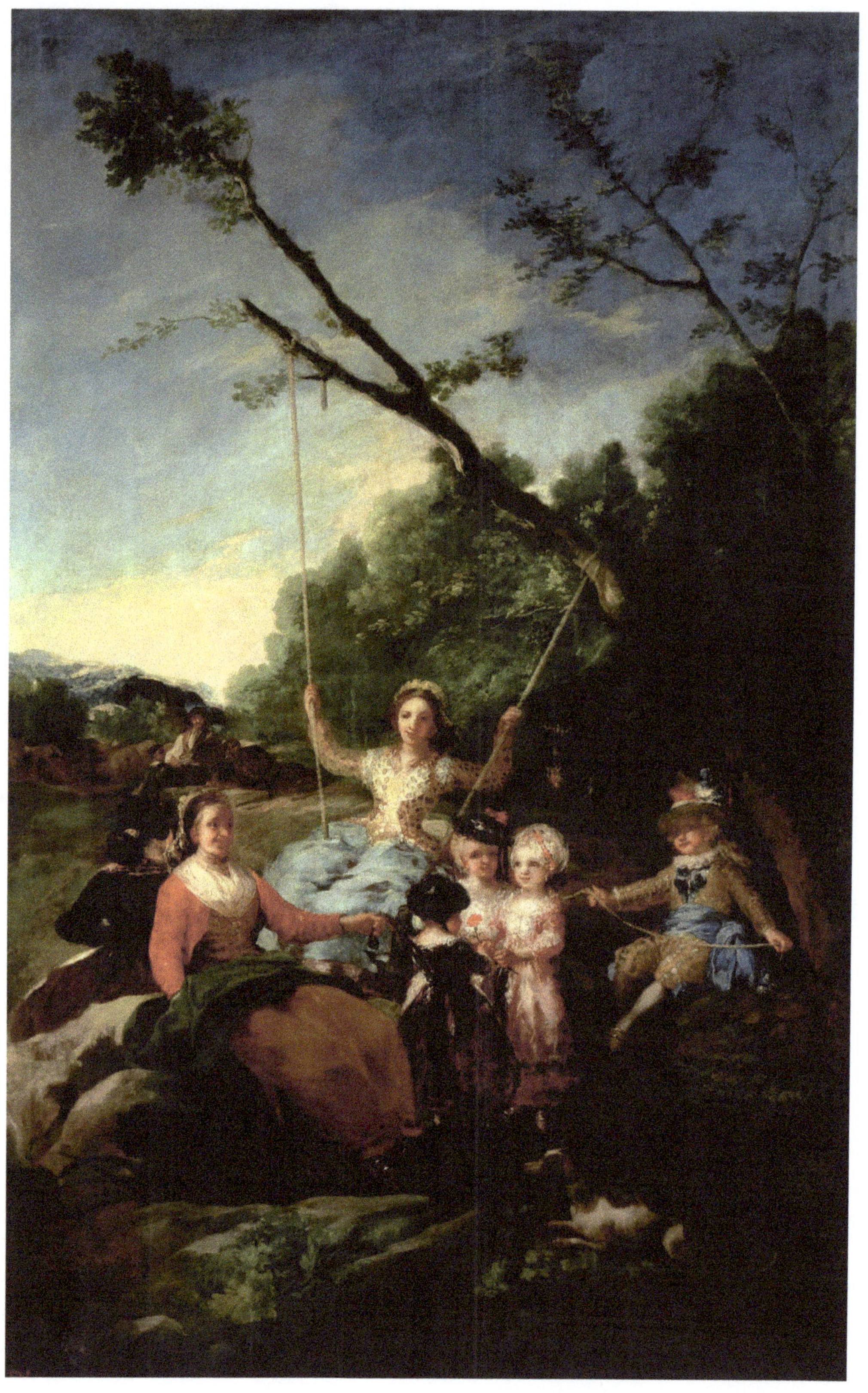

FRANCISCO de GOYA y LUCIENTES

(Fuendetodos, 1746 – Bordeaux, 1828)

Goya is perhaps the most approachable of painters. His art, like his life, is an open book. He concealed nothing from his contemporaries, and offered his art to them with the same frankness. The entrance to his world is not barricaded with technical difficulties. He proved that if a man has the capacity to live and multiply his experiences, to fight and work, he can produce great art without classical decorum and traditional respectability. He was born in 1746, in Fuendetodos, a small Spanish mountain village of a hundred inhabitants. As a child he worked in the fields with his two brothers and his sister until his talent for drawing put an end to his misery. At fourteen, supported by a wealthy patron, he went to Saragossa to study with a court painter and later, when he was nineteen, on to Madrid.

Up to his thirty-seventh year, if we leave out of account the tapestry cartoons of unheralded decorative quality and five small pictures, Goya painted nothing of any significance, but once in control of his refractory powers, he produced masterpieces with the speed of Rubens. His court appointment was followed by a decade of incessant activity – years of painting and scandal, with intervals of bad health.

Goya's etchings demonstrate a draughtsmanship of the first rank. In paint, like Velázquez, he is more or less dependent on the model, but not in the detached fashion of the expert in still-life. If a woman was ugly, he made her a despicable horror; if she was alluring, he dramatised her charm. He preferred to finish his portraits at one sitting and was a tyrant with his models. Like Velázquez too, he concentrated on faces, but he drew his heads cunningly, and constructed them out of tones of transparent greys. Monstrous forms inhabit his black-and-white world; these are his most profoundly deliberated productions. His fantastic figures, as he called them, fill us with a sense of ignoble joy, aggravate our devilish instincts and delight us with the uncharitable ecstasies of destruction. His genius attained its highest point in his etchings on the horrors of war. When placed beside the work of Goya, other pictures of war pale into sentimental studies of cruelty. He avoided the scattered action of the battlefield, and confined himself to isolated scenes of butchery. Nowhere else did he display such mastery of form and movement, such dramatic gestures and appalling effects of light and darkness? In all directions Goya renewed and innovated.

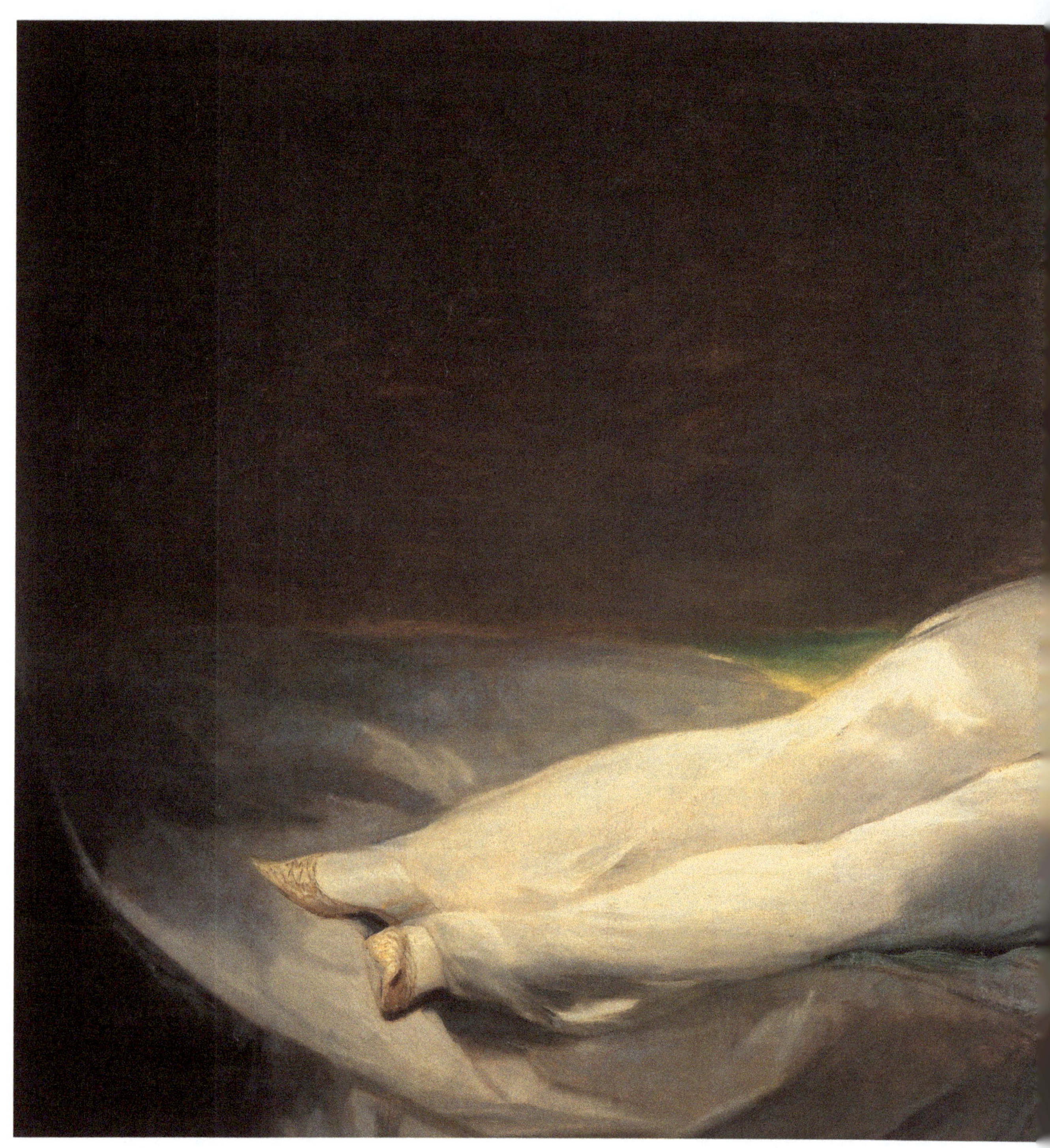

▲ **Francisco de Goya y Lucientes**,
The Swing, 1779.
Oil on canvas, 260 x 165 cm.
Museo Nacional del Prado, Madrid.

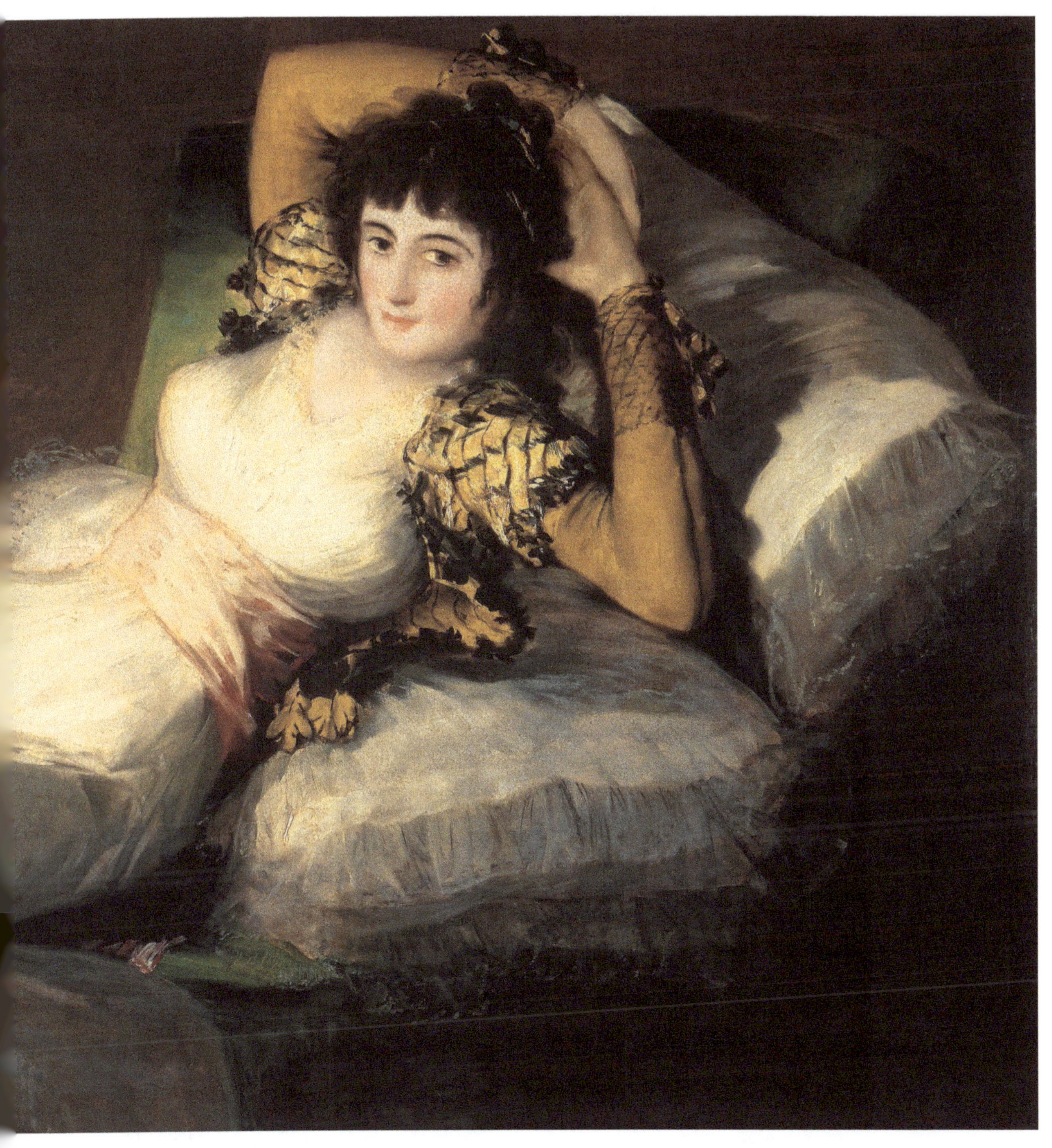

▲ **Francisco de Goya y Lucientes**,
The Clothed Maja, 1800-1803.
Oil on canvas, 97 x 190 cm.
Museo Nacional del Prado, Madrid.

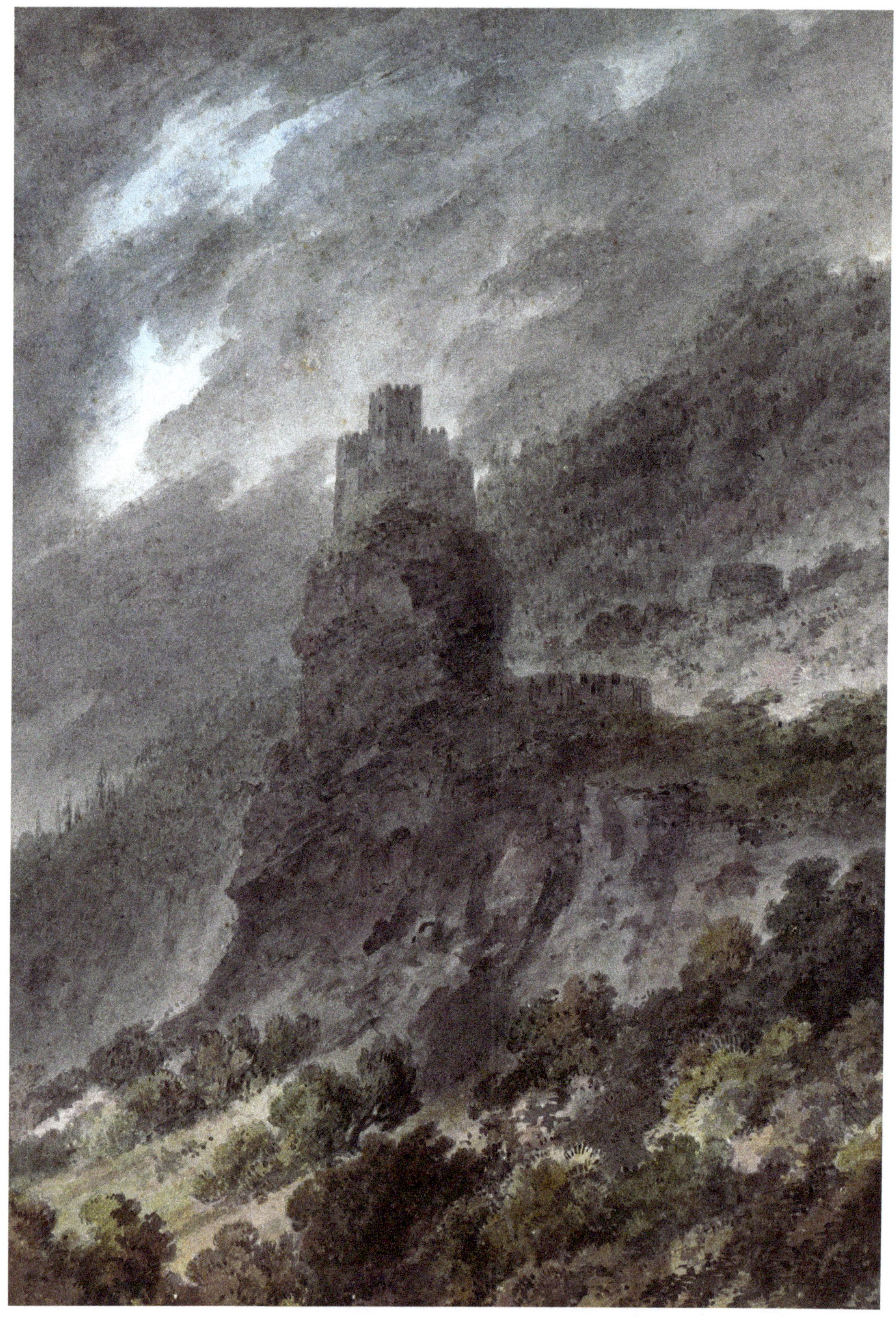

JOHN ROBERT COZENS

(London, 1752-1797)

As the son of the Russian-born watercolourist Alexander Cozens, is it not surprising that John Robert Cozens exhibited some early works with the Society of Artists at the age of fifteen. He was taught by his father, and between 1776 and 1779 he travelled in Switzerland and Italy with the scholar and connoisseur Richard Payne Knight, painting many watercolour Alpine views and Italian landscapes such as A Cavern in the Campagna, Rome (in the Victoria & Albert Museum). He returned to England in 1779 and lived in Bath, where he enjoyed some success with the works he had executed on the continent, making and selling numerous copies. He travelled again to Italy in 1782 with the writer (and later politician) William Beckford, who was then one of his patrons. Cozens made many sketches during the trip, which came to an end when an outbreak of malaria struck the party, including the artist himself. He recovered in Portici in the home of Sir William Hamilton, a British diplomat.

From 1793 Cozens began to suffer from severe mental illness, and had a breakdown in 1794 which resulted in him being placed in the care of a Dr Thomas Monro for the last few years of his life. This doctor made several of Cozens' works available for study by art students, which had great influence on such artists as J. M. W. Turner and Thomas Girtin. Cozens was buried in London on New Year's Day 1798.

Cozens' works are filled with a quiet majesty and a sense of vastness. The painter John Constable described Cozens as "the greatest genius that ever touched landscape", and stated that his watercolours were "all poetry".

◀ **John Robert Cozens,**
View of a Castle between Bolzano and Trent, 18th century.
Watercolour on canvas.
Victoria & Albert Museum, London.

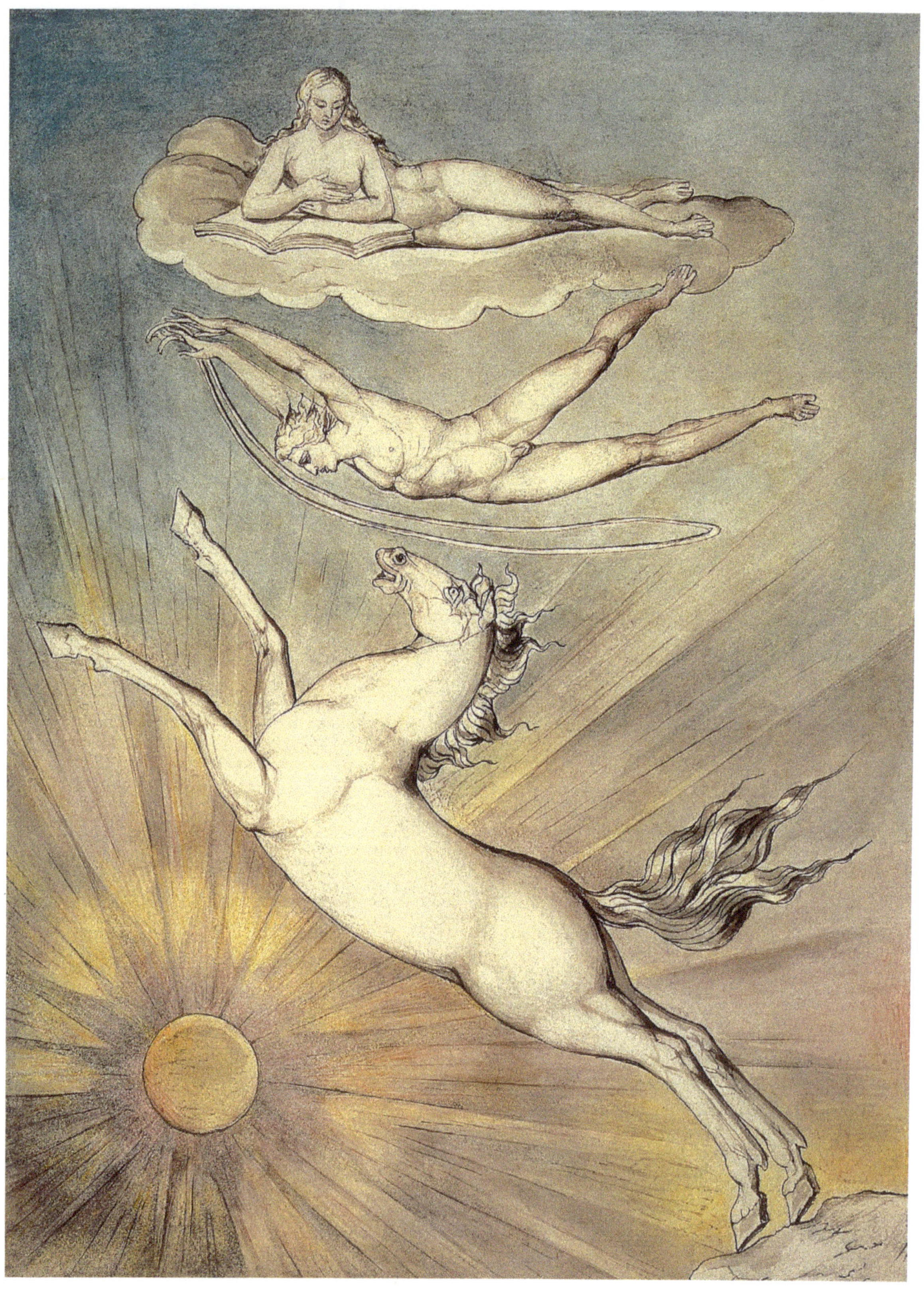

WILLIAM BLAKE

(London, 1757-1827)

Poet, draughtsman, engraver and painter, William Blake's work is made up of several elements – Gothic art, Germanic reverie, the Bible, Milton and Shakespeare – to which were added Dante and a certain taste for linear designs, resembling geometric diagrams, and relates him to the great classical movement inspired by Winckelmann and propagated by David. This is the sole point of contact discernible between the classicism of David and English art, though furtive and indirect. Blake is the most mystic of the English painters, perhaps the only true mystic. He was ingenious in his inner imagination, and his interpretations of ancient and modern poets reveal as true and candid a spirit as the title of his first work – poems he composed, illustrated and set to music, *Songs of Innocence* and *Songs of Experience*. Later he achieved grandeur, power and profundity, especially in certain tempera paintings. Just like others, Blake was considered an eccentric by most of his contemporaries, until his genius was recognised in the second half of the nineteenth century.

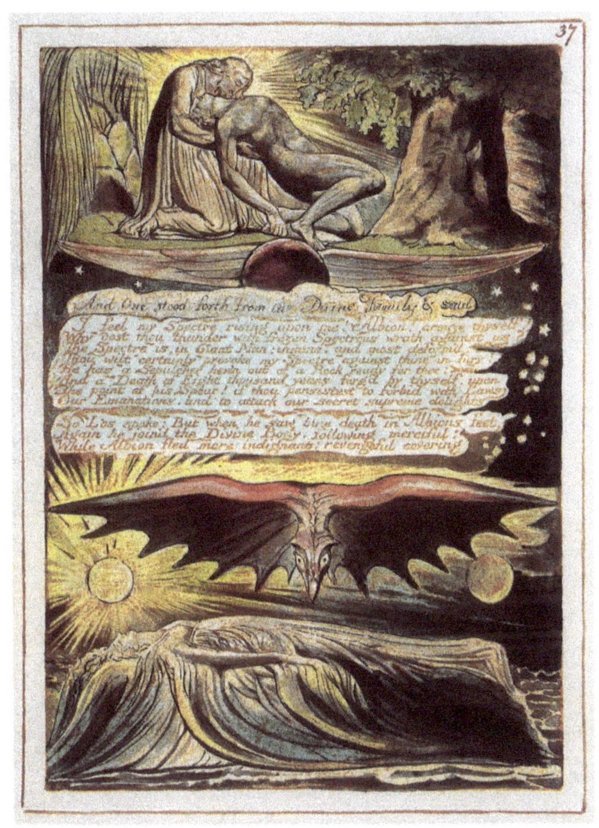

▲ **William Blake**,
Plate from Jerusalem, The Emanation of the Giant Albion,
1804.
Etching and watercolour.
Yale Center for British Art, New Haven.

◀ **William Blake**,
The Genius of Shakespeare, 1809.
Feather and watercolour on paper, 30.8 x 19.1 cm.
The British Museum, London.

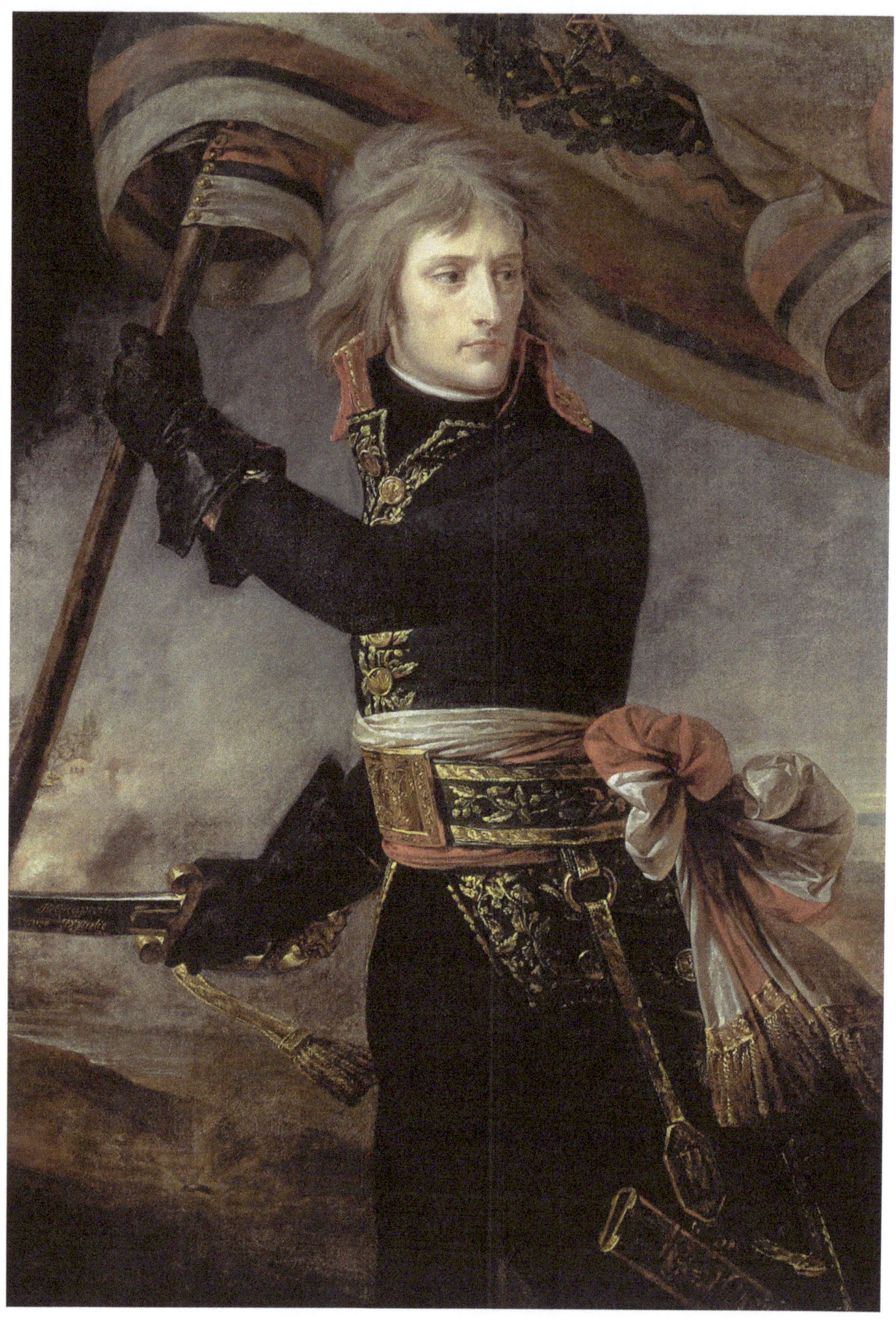

ANTOINE JEAN GROS, BARON GROS

(Paris, 1771-1835)

Gros's father, who was a miniaturist, began to teach him to draw at the age of six. Towards the end of 1785 Gros chose to enter Jacques-Louis David's studio, which he frequented assiduously, at the same time attending classes at the Collège Mazarin. In 1791, the death of his father, who had fallen on hard times during the Revolution, threw Gros upon his own resources. He now devoted himself wholly to his profession, and in 1792 competed for the *Grand Prix*, but was unsuccessful. About this time, however, on the recommendation of the École des beaux-arts, he was employed to paint the portraits of the members of the Convention. When the development of the Revolution meant that in 1793 Gros had to leave France for Italy, he supported himself in Genoa by the same means, producing a great quantity of miniatures. On the 15th November 1796, Gros was present with the army near Arcola when Bonaparte planted the tricolour on the bridge. Gros painted this moment, and showed from his treatment of

it that he had found his vocation. Bonaparte at once gave him the post of "inspecteur aux revues", which enabled him to follow the army.

In 1799, having escaped from the besieged city of Genoa, Gros made his way to Paris, and in the beginning of 1801 took up his quarters in the Capucins. His esquisse (Musée de Nantes) of the *Battle of Nazareth* won the prize offered in 1802 by the consuls, but he never received it, owing, it is said, to the jealousy Napoleon felt for Junot. However the First Consul made up for this by commissioning Gros to paint his own visit to the pesthouse of Jaffa. *Bonaparte visiting the Plague-Stricken in Jaffa* (11th March 1799) (Louvre) was followed by *the Battle of Akoubir, 25th July 1799* in 1806 (Versailles), and Napoleon on the *Field of the Battle of Eylau* (9th February 1807) in 1808 (Louvre). These three subjects – the popular leader facing the pestilence unmoved, challenging the splendid instant of victory, heart-sick with the bitter cost of a hard-won field – made Gros famous. Gros was decorated and named Baron of the Empire by Napoleon.

Trained in the style of the Classicists, he was shackled by their rules, even when – by his

◀ **Antoine Jean Gros,**
Napoleon Bonaparte on Arcole Bridge, November 17, 1796, 1796.
Oil on canvas, 130 x 94 cm.
Musée national du château et des Trianons, Versailles.

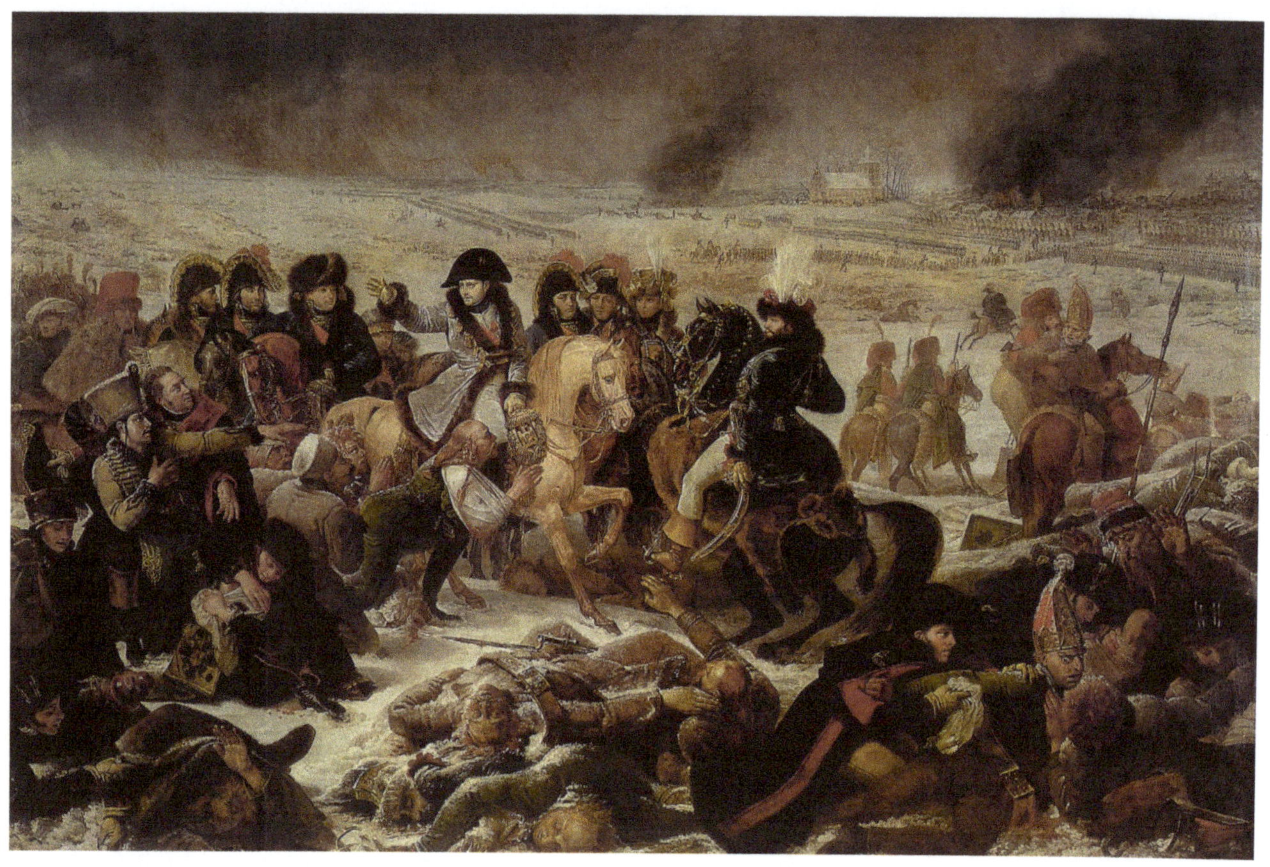

naturalistic treatment of subjects, and use of picturesque effect in colour and tone – he seemed to run counter to them. In 1810 his *Capitulation of Madrid, 4th December 1808* and *Battle of the Pyramids, 21st July 1798* (Versailles) show that his star had deserted him. His *Francis I* and *Charles V at the Abbey of Saint-Denis* of 1812 (Louvre) had considerable success, but the decoration of the dome of the church of St Geneviève (begun in 1811 and completed in 1824), now the Pantheon, is the only work of Gros's later years which shows his early force and vigour. *The Departure of Louis XVIII from the Palais des Tuileries, night of the 20th March 1815* (Versailles), the *Embarkation of the Duchess of Angoulême at Pouillac* (Bordeaux), the ceiling of the Egyptian room in the Louvre, and finally his *Hercules and Diomedes*, exhibited in 1835, demonstrate that Gros's efforts – in accordance with the advice of his old master, David – to stem the rising tide of Romanticism, served only to damage his once brilliant reputation. Exasperated by criticism and the consciousness of failure, Gros sought refuge in the unrefined. On the 25th June 1835 he was found drowned on the shores of the Seine near Sèvres. From a paper which he had placed in his hat it became known that "tired of life, and betrayed by last faculties which rendered it bearable, he had resolved to end it".

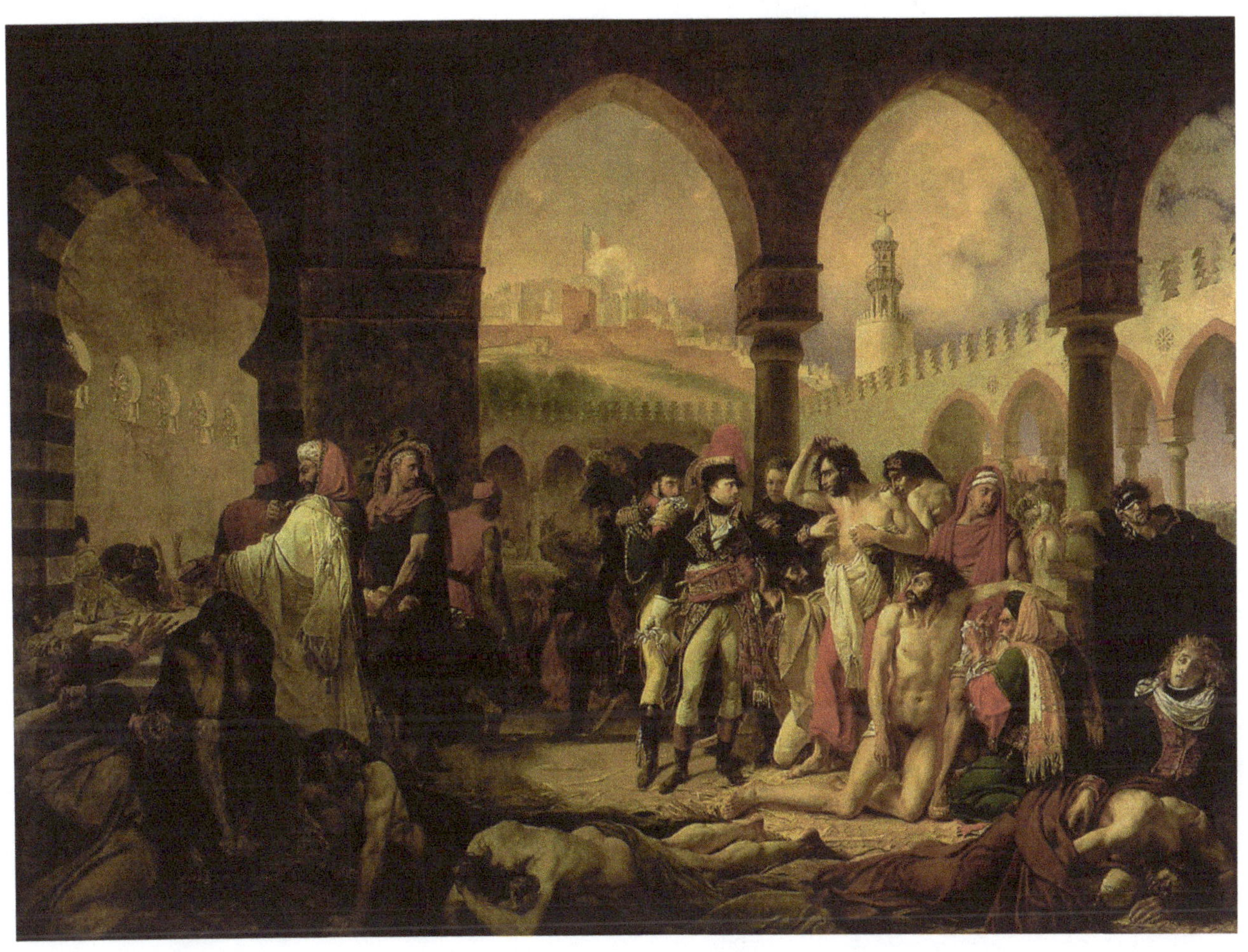

◄ Antoine Jean Gros,
Napoleon on the Battlefield of Eylau (February 9, 1807), 1808.
Oil on canvas, 521 x 784 cm.
Musée du Louvre, Paris.

▲ Antoine Jean Gros,
Bonaparte Visiting the Plague House at Jaffa, 1804.
Oil on canvas, 523 x 715 cm.
Musée du Louvre, Paris.

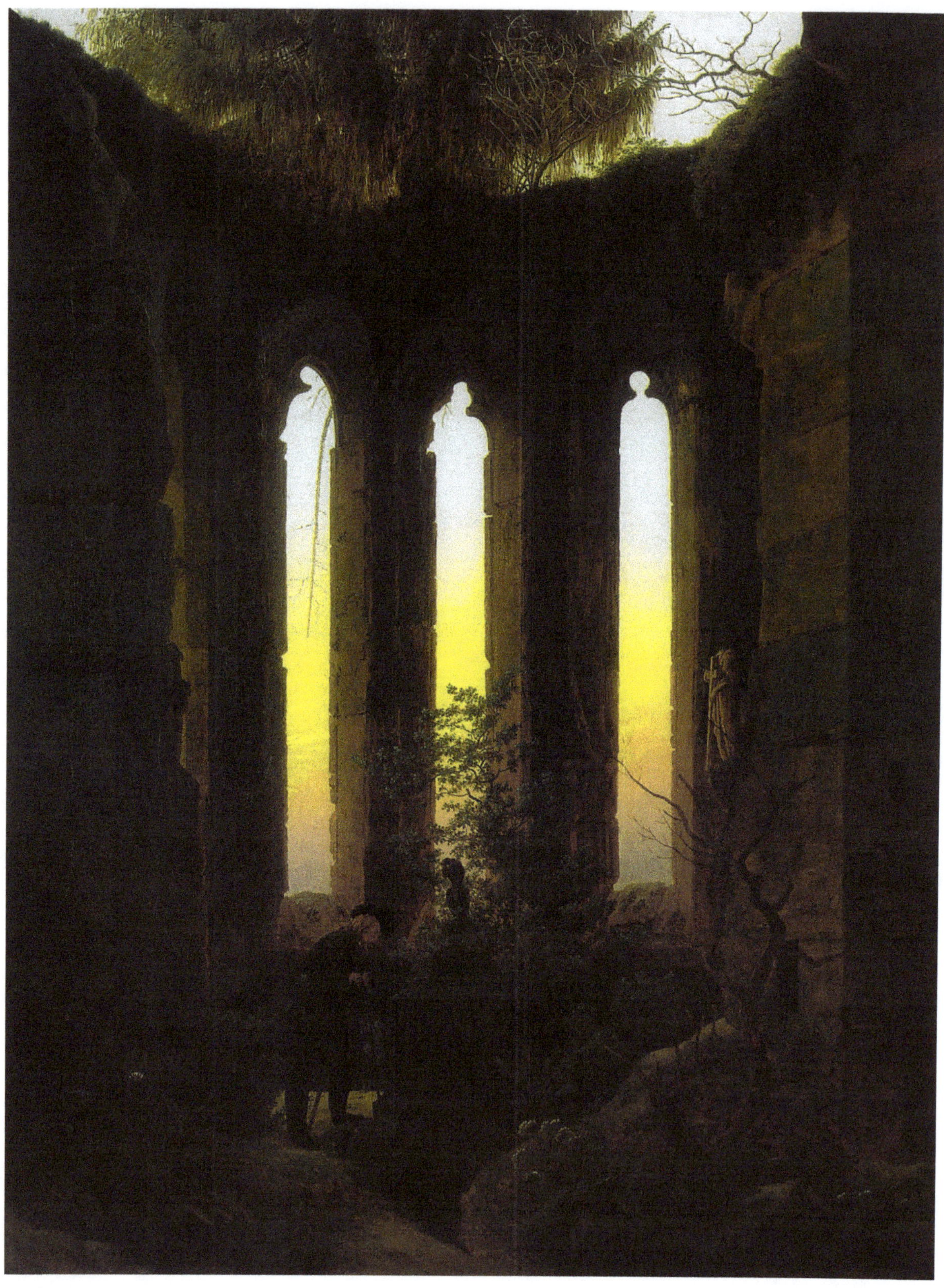

CASPAR DAVID FRIEDRICH

(Greiswald, 1774 – Dresden, 1840)

L ike Gainsborough, Friedrich is mostly known for his landscapes. They depict trees, hills, and misty mornings based on his observation of nature. Mountains symbolise an immovable faith while the trees are an allegory of hope. Therefore his landscapes reflect his spiritual relationship with nature and his religious aspirations. His Monk by the Sea expresses his recurring theme of the insignificance of the individual in relation to the vastness of nature. A draughtsman and printmaker as well as a painter, he was one of the greatest German leaders of Romanticism.

Friedrich was born into a strict Lutheran family and was to a great extent self-taught. He studied at the Academy in Copenhagen between 1794 and 1798 before moving to Dresden, where he met Philipp Otto Runge, another significant German Romantic painter. His early works were in watercolour or ink, but at a later stage he moved on to oil painting, probably not until after the age of thirty. He depicted the landscapes of northern Germany, closely observing the light and atmosphere of this particular environment. He painted one of his most controversial works in 1808, *The Cross in the Mountains*, an altarpiece showing a cross rising out of a rocky peak surrounded by trees, almost silhouetted against an evening sky, the setting sun's rays forming a natural halo.

One of Friedrich's most famous paintings, and the one that seems to most remind viewers of the essence of Romanticism, is of course *The Wanderer above the Sea of Fog*, painted in 1818. A man stands on a rocky peak, his back to the viewer, gazing out at a sea of cloud. Mountains loom out of the mist, and the feeling of awe inspired by the power of nature was characteristic of the sublime aspect central to Romanticism. In 1835 Friedrich suffered a stroke, which resulted in a paralysis that meant he could never paint again, and he died five years later.

◀ **Caspar David Friedrich**,
The Tomb of Ulrich von Hutten, 1824.
Oil on canvas, 93.5 x 73.4 cm.
Staatliche Kunstsammlungen, Weimar.

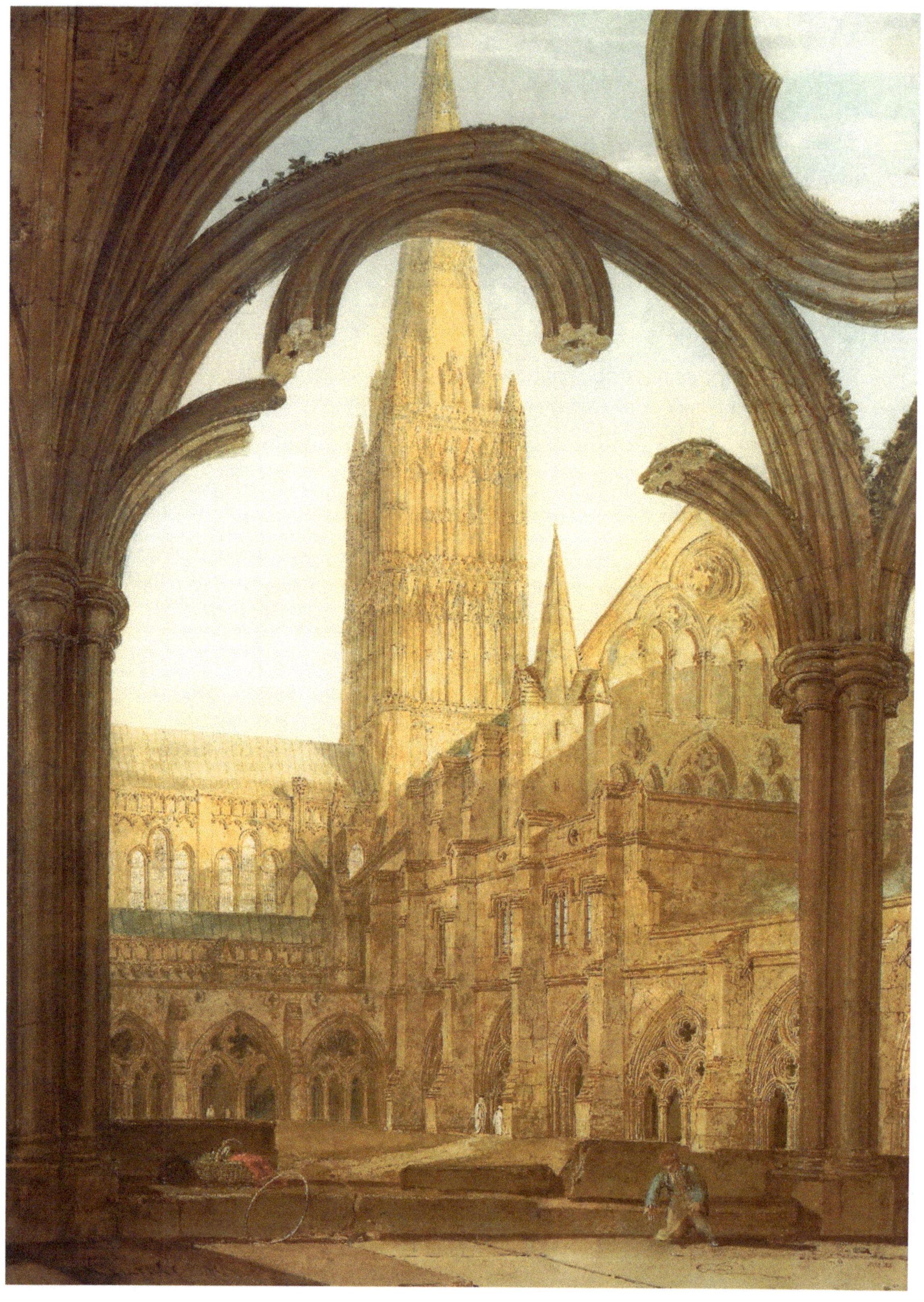

JOSEP M. W. TURNER

(London, 1775-1851)

At fifteen, Turner was already exhibiting his View of Lambeth. He soon acquired the reputation of an immensely clever watercolourist. A disciple of Girtin and Cozens, he showed in his choice and presentation of theme a picturesque imagination which seemed to mark him out for a brilliant career as an illustrator. He travelled, first in his native land and then on several occasions in France, the Rhine Valley, Switzerland and Italy. He soon began to look beyond illustration. However, even in works in which we are tempted to see only picturesque imagination, there appears his dominant and guiding ideal of lyric landscape. His choice of a single master from the past is an eloquent witness, for he studied profoundly such canvases of Claude as he could find in England, copying and imitating them with a marvellous degree of perfection. His cult for the great painter never failed. He desired his *Sun rising through Vapour* and *Dido building Carthage* to be placed in the National Gallery side by side with two of Claude's masterpieces. And there we may still see them and judge how legitimate was this proud and splendid homage. It was only in 1819 that Turner went to Italy, to go again in 1829 and 1840. Certainly Turner experienced emotions and found subjects for reverie there which he later translated in terms of his own genius into symphonies of light and colour. Ardour is tempered with melancholy, as shadow strives with light. Melancholy, even as it appears in the enigmatic and profound creation of Albrecht Dürer, finds no home in Turner's protean fairyland – what place could it have in a cosmic dream? Humanity does not appear there, except perhaps as stage characters at whom we hardly glance. Turner's pictures fascinate us and yet we think of nothing precise, nothing human, only unforgettable colours and phantoms that lay hold on our imaginations. Humanity really only inspired him when linked with the idea of death – a strange death, more a lyrical dissolution – like the finale of an opera.

◀ **Joseph M. W. Turner,**
South View of Salisbury Cathedral from the Cloister, c. 1802.
Watercolour, 68 x 49.6 cm.
Victoria & Albert Museum, London.

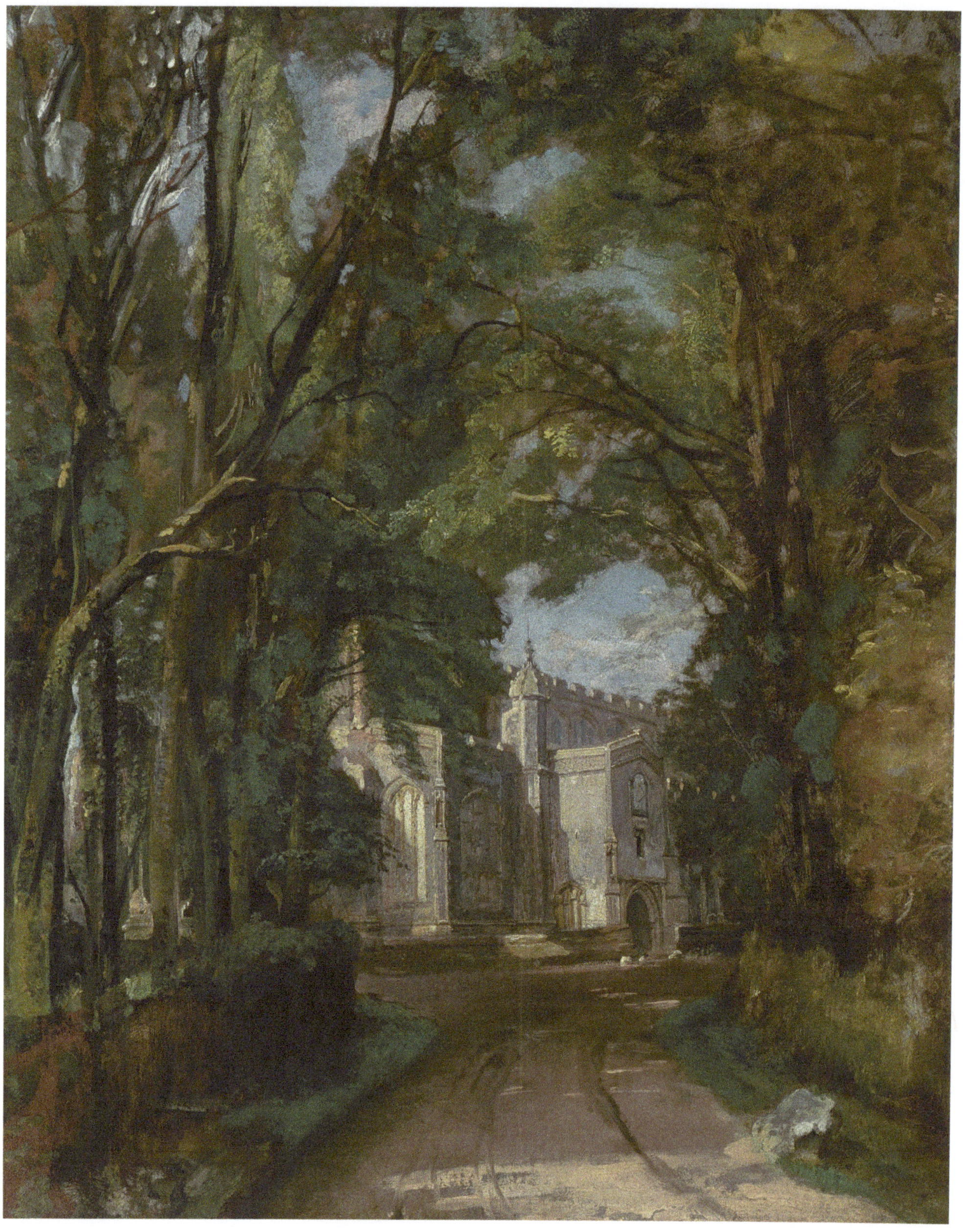

JOHN CONSTABLE

(East Bergholt, 1776 – London, 1837)

John Constable was the first English landscape painter to take no lessons from the Dutch. He is instead indebted to the landscapes of Rubens, but his real model was Gainsborough, whose landscapes, with great trees planted in well-balanced masses on land sloping upwards towards the frame, have a rhythm often found in Rubens. Constable's originality does not lie in his choice of subjects, which frequently repeated themes beloved by Gainsborough.

Nevertheless, Constable seems to belong to a new century; he ushered in a new era. The difference in his approach results both from technique and feeling. Except for the French, Constable was the first landscape painter to consider as a primary and essential task the sketch made directly from nature at a single sitting; an idea which contains in essence the destinies of modern landscape, and perhaps of most modern painting. It is this momentary 'impression' of all the things which will be the soul of the future work. Working at leisure upon the large canvas, an artist's aim is to enrich and complete the sketch while retaining its pristine freshness. These are the two processes to which Constable devoted himself, while discovering the exuberant abundance of life in the simplest of country places. He had the palette of a creative colourist and a technique of vivid hatchings heralding that of the French Impressionists. He audaciously and frankly introduced green into painting, the green of lush meadows, the green of summer foliage, all the greens which, until then, painters had refused to see except through bluish, yellow, or – more often – brown spectacles.

Of the great landscape painters who occupied so important a place in nineteenth-century art, Corot was probably the only one to escape the influence of Constable. All the others are more or less direct descendants of the master of East Bergholt.

◄ **John Constable**,
East Bergholt Church, 19th century.
Oil on canvas.
Private collection.

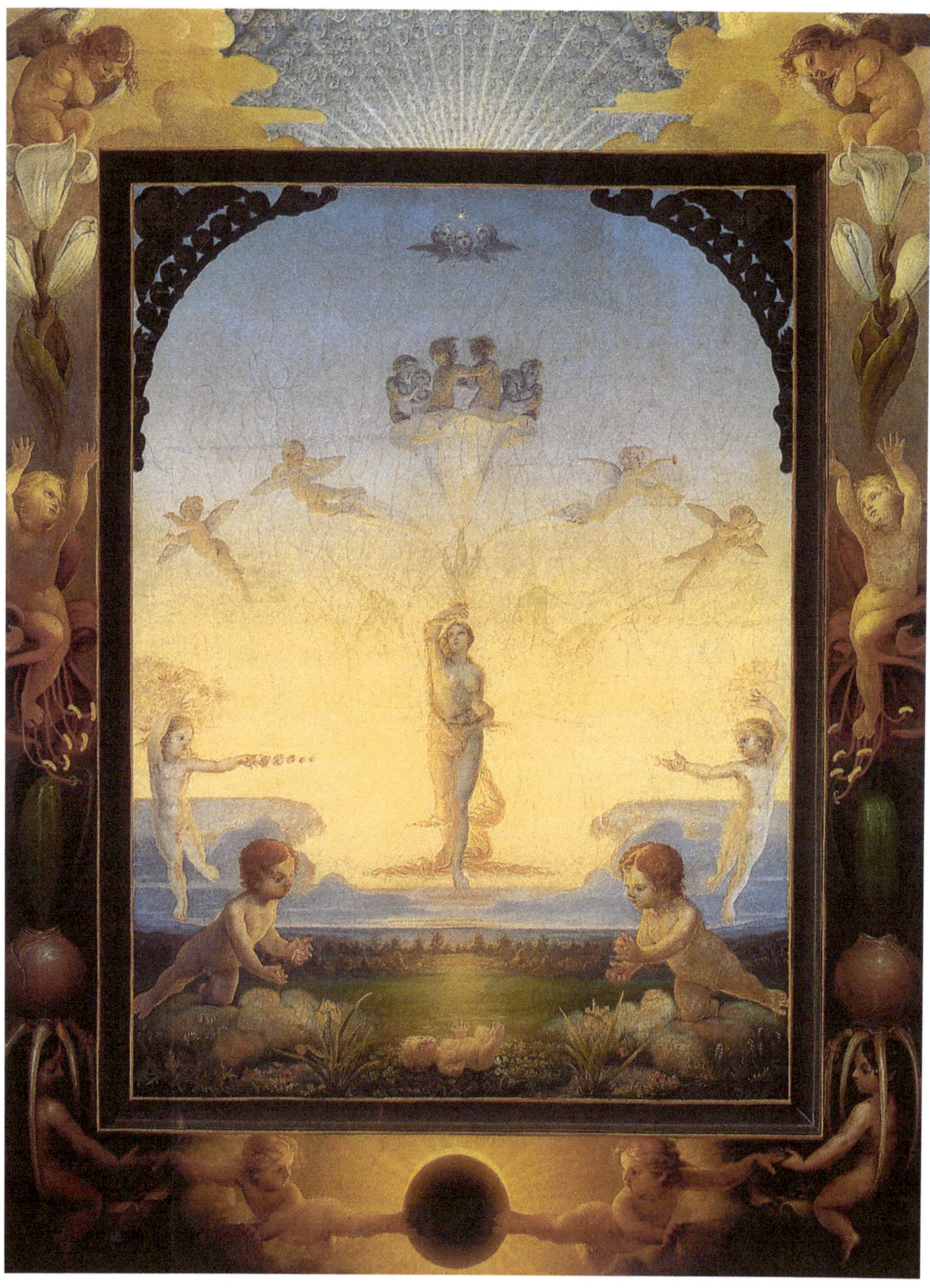

PHILIPP OTTO RUNGE

(Walgast, 1777 – Hamburg, 1810)

The German Romantic painter Runge moved from his hometown to Hamburg at the age of eighteen, where he worked for his brother Daniel. His brother later gave him an allowance so that he could practise his art as he wanted. Runge studied painting in Hamburg and later at the Copenhagen Academy before moving to Dresden. There he met Caspar David Friedrich and the pair became friends. He married Pauline Bassenge in 1804, and the couple returned to Hamburg. Runge's major paintings were executed at this time, among them *The Nightingale's Lesson*, *Rest on the Flight into Egypt*, *The Artist's Parents*, The Hülsenbeck Children and two versions of Morning. As time went on, Runge moved away from history painting towards landscape painting, and he proved to be of great influence on the English Romanticists. He died young, at the age of just thirty-three, with his major work Die *Tageszeiten* (Times of Day) unfinished. This was a cycle of huge compositions which was designed to be hung in a particular architectural environment and viewed with poetry and music, which embodied the Romantic concept of *Gesamtkunstwerk* – "total art". The designs for this work were engraved in 1805, and were the only pieces by him really known to the public during his lifetime. Just before he died of tuberculosis he created The *Colour Sphere*, an extended and developed three-dimensional version of the colour wheel, which organised the colours by hue, brightness and saturation.

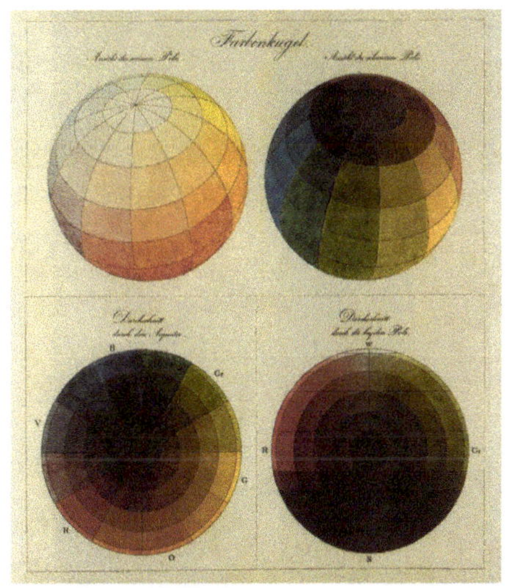

◀ **Philipp Otto Runge**,
Morning (first version), 1808.
Oil on canvas, 108.9 x 85.4 cm.
Hamburger Kunsthalle, Hamburg.

▲ **Philipp Otto Runge**,
Farbenkugel (Colour Sphere), 1809.
Engraving painted with watercolours, 22.5 x 18.9 cm.
Hamburger Kunsthalle, Hamburg.

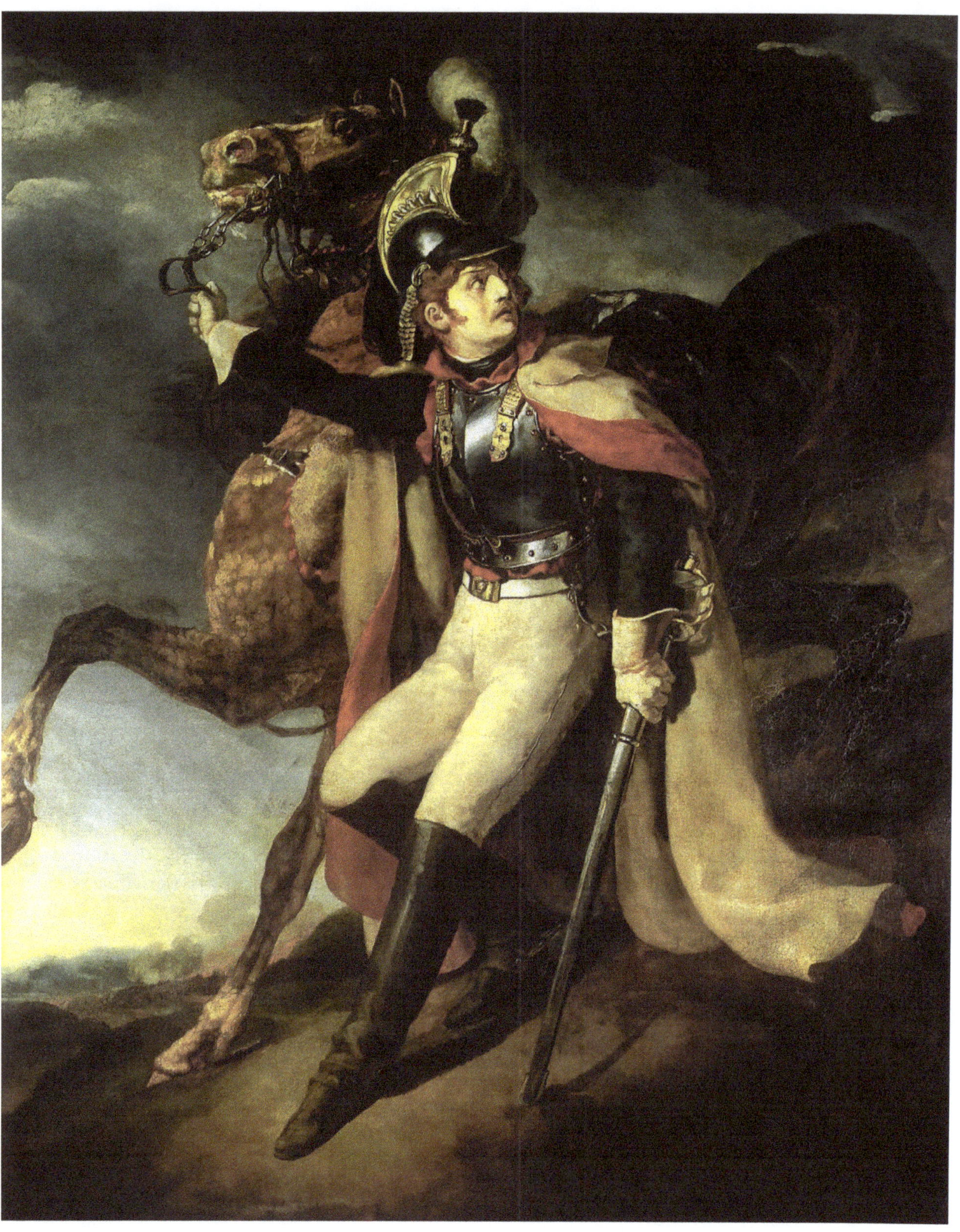

THÉODORE GÉRICAULT

(Rouen, 1791 – Paris 1824)

Théodore Géricault, was born in Rouen in 1791. In 1808 he entered the studio of Charles Vernet, from where, in 1810, he moved to that of Guérin, whom he drove to despair with his passion for Rubens and the unorthodox manner in which he persisted in interpreting nature. At the Salon of 1812 Géricault attracted attention with his *Officer of the Hussars* (Louvre), a work in which he depicted the cavalry in the hour of its triumph, and demonstrated the solid training received from Guérin in rendering a picturesque point of view which was in itself a protest against the cherished convictions of the neoclassical school. Two years later, in 1814, he re-exhibited this work accompanied by the reverse picture, *The Wounded Cuirassier* (Louvre) and in both subjects drew attention to contemporary life, treated neglected types of living form, and exhibited that mastery of and delight in the horse that was such a feature of his work. Disconcerted by the tempest of contradictory opinion which arose over these two pictures, Géricault gave way to his enthusiasm for horses and soldiers and enrolled in *the mousquetaires*. During the Hundred Days he followed the king to Béthune, but, on his regiment being disbanded, he eagerly returned to his profession. He left France for Italy in 1816, and in Rome nobly depicted his favourite animal in his great painting *Free Horses racing in Rome*. Returning to Paris, Géricault exhibited *The Raft of the Medusa* (Louvre) at the Salon of 1819. This subject not only enabled him to prove his zealous and scientific study of the human form, but contained those elements of the heroic and pathetic that existed in modern life, to which he had appealed in his earliest productions.

Easily depressed or elated, Géricault took the hostility that this work excited to heart, and went on to spend nearly two years in London, where *The Raft of the Medusa* was exhibited with success. At the end of 1822 he was again in Paris, and produced a great quantity of projects for vast compositions, models in wax, and a flayed horse as a preliminary to an equestrian statue. His health was by then in decline due to various excesses, and on the 26th January 1824 he died at the age of thirty-three.

◀ **Théodore Géricault**,
The Wounded Cuirassier, 1814.
Oil on canvas, 358 x 294 cm.
Musée du Louvre, Paris.

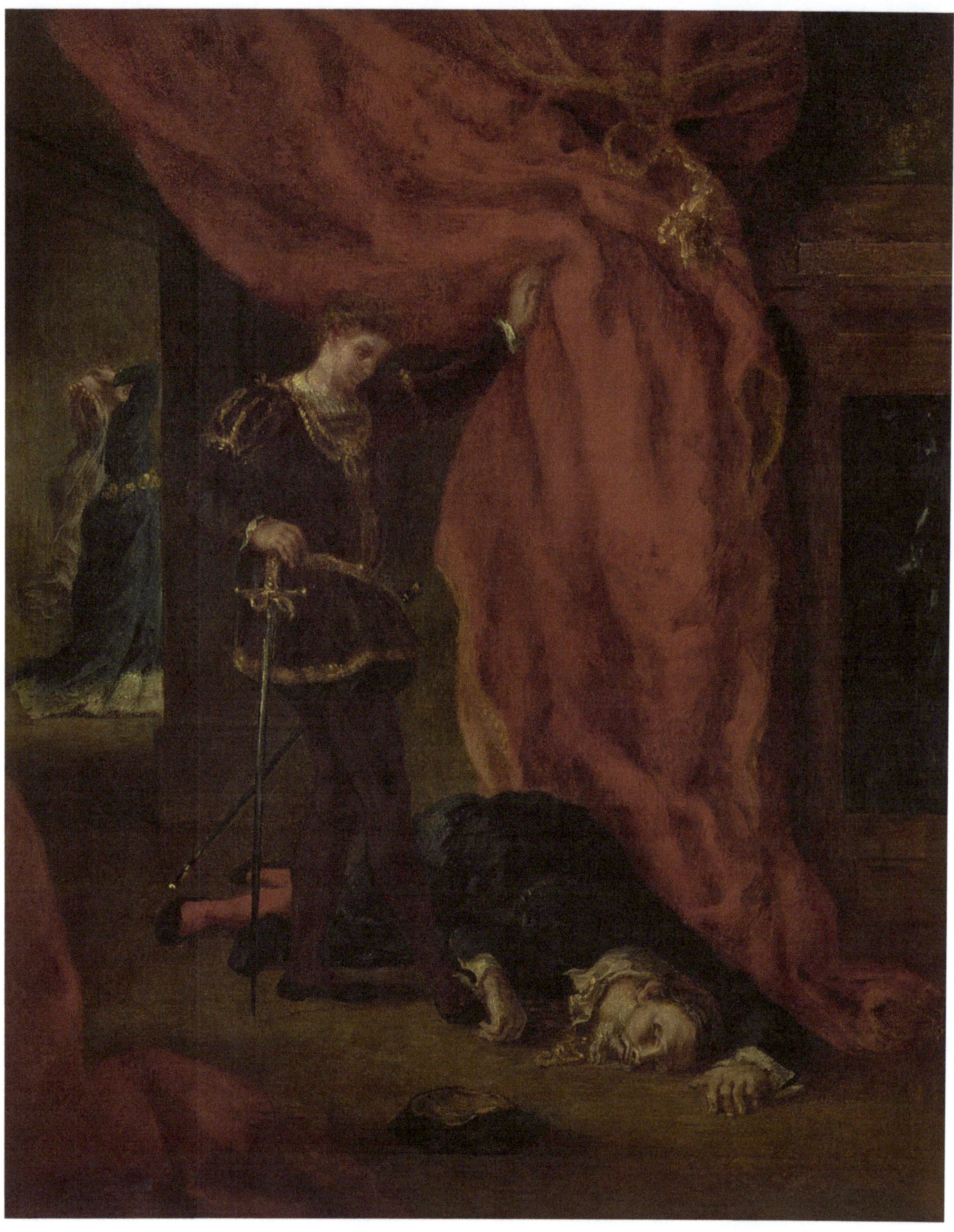

EUGÈNE DELACROIX

(Saint-Maurice, 1798 – Paris, 1863)

Ferdinand Victor Eugène Delacroix (known as Eugène Delacroix) was one of the greatest colourists of the nineteenth century, in the sense of one who thinks and feels and expresses himself by means of colours and sees them in his mind's eye as a composition, before he begins to resolve the whole into its parts, and work out the separate details of form.

He nurtured his talent through the works of the colourists in the Louvre, especially Rubens. Indirectly it came out of the heart of the Romantic movement which had spread over Europe. Delacroix was inspired by the writers Goethe, Scott, Byron, and Victor Hugo. His own romantic nature flamed up through contact with theirs; he was possessed with their souls and became the first of the Romantic painters. He took many of his subjects from the poets of his preference, not to translate into literal illustrations, but to make them express in his own language of painting the most agitated emotions of the human heart.

On the other hand it is generally in the relationship of several figures, in other words in drama, that Delacroix finds the natural and striking expression of his ideas. His work is an immense and multiform poem, at once lyrical and dramatic, about passions – the violent and murderous passions which fascinate, dominate, and rend humanity. In the elaboration and execution of the pages of this poem, Delacroix does not forego any of his faculties as a man and an artist of vast intelligence standing on a level with the thoughts of the greatest in history, legend and poetry.

Rather, he makes use of a feverish imagination always controlled by lucid reasoning and cool willpower. His expressive and life-like drawing, strong and subtle colour, sometimes composing a bitter harmony, sometimes overcast by that "sulphurous" note already observed by contemporaries, produce an atmosphere of storm, supplication, and anguish. Passion, movement and drama must not be supposed to engender disorder. With Delacroix as with Rubens, there hovers over the saddest representations, over tumults, horrors and massacre, a kind of serenity which is the sign of art itself and the mark of a mind that is master of its subject.

◀ **Eugène Delacroix,**
Hamlet before the Body of Polonius, 1855.
Oil on canvas.
Musée des Beaux-Arts, Reims.

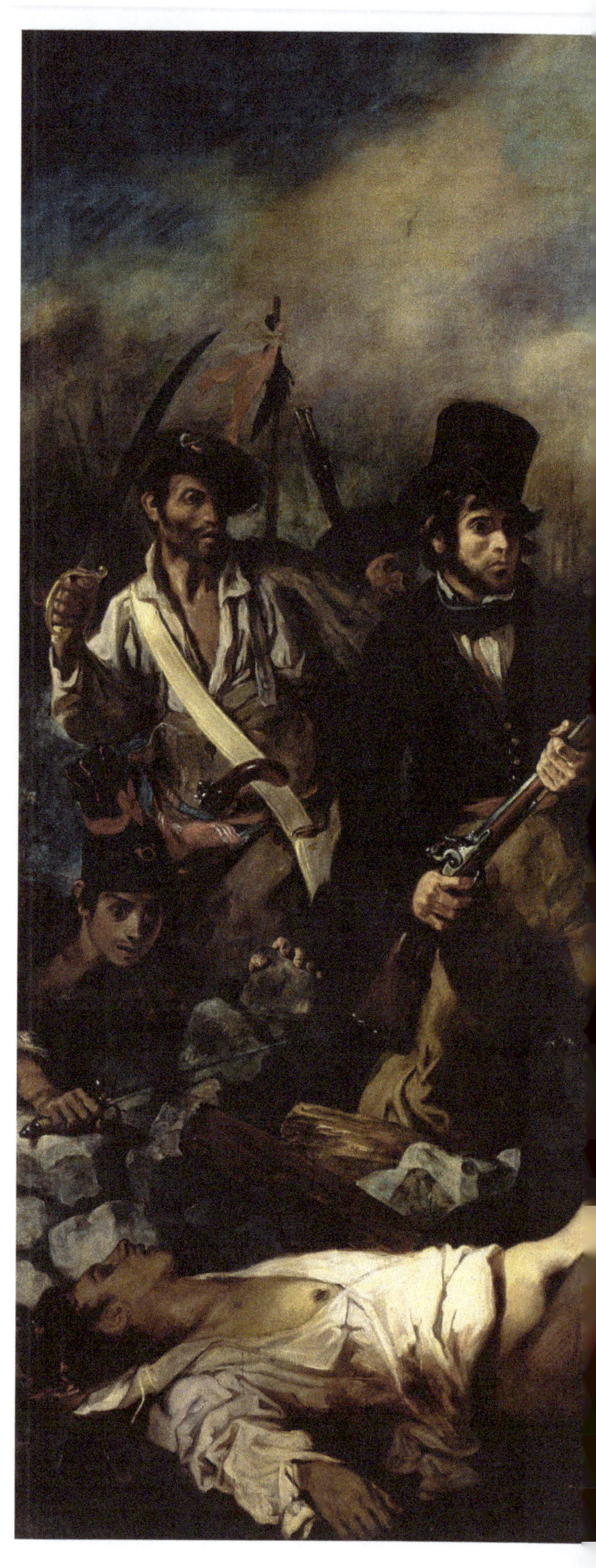

Eugène Delacroix, ▶
Liberty Leading the People (28th July 1830), 1830.
Oil on canvas, 260 x 325 cm.
Musée du Louvre, Paris.

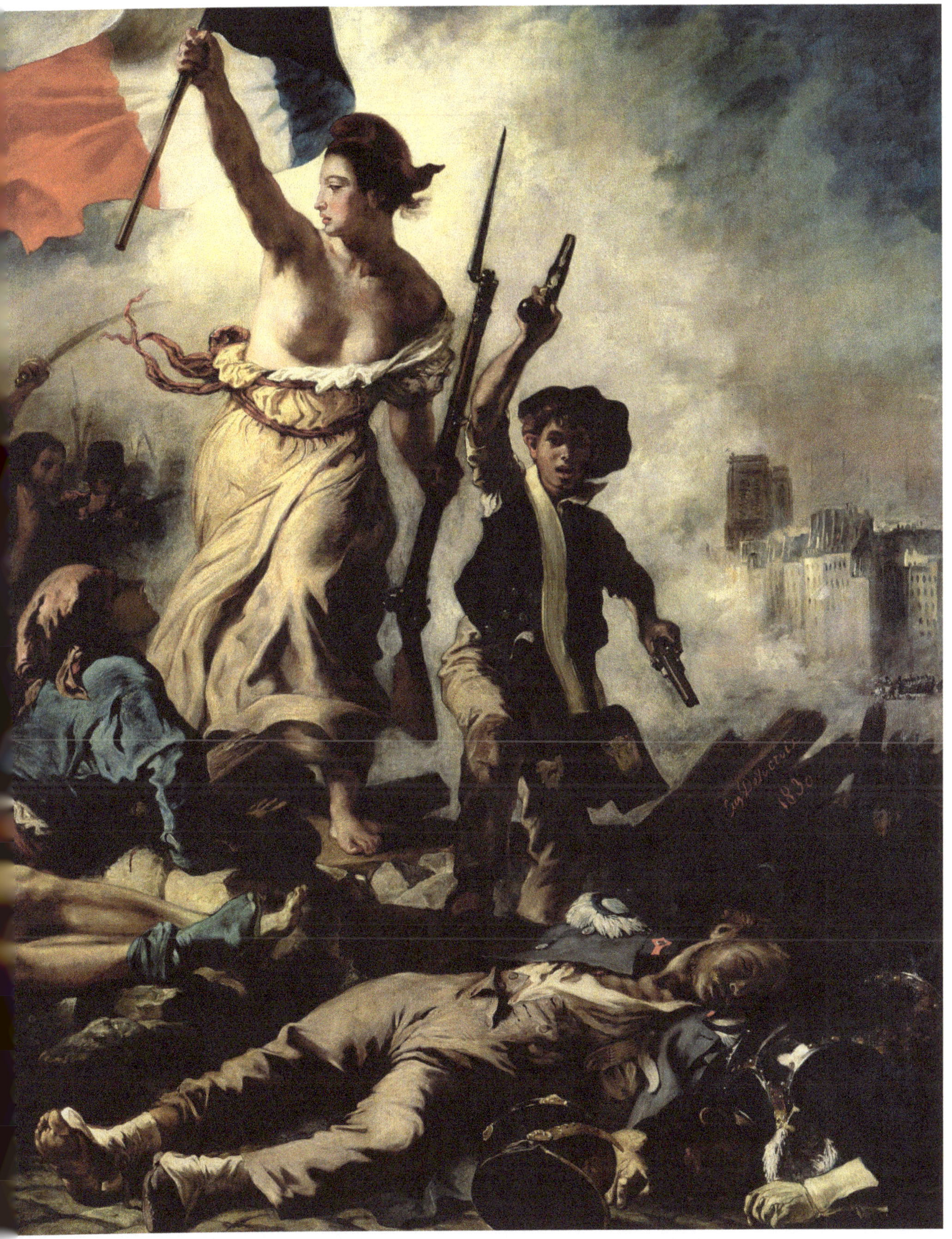

LIST OF ILLUSTRATIONS

ART HISTORY COLLECTION

Abstract Art	Naive Art
Art Deco	Neoclassicism
Art Nouveau	Persian Art
Baroque	Post-Impressionism
Byzantine Art	Realism
Chinese Art	Renaissance
Cubism	Pre-Raphaelites
Dada	Rococo
Early Italian Art	Roman Art
Egypt Art	Romanesque Art
Expressionism	Romanticism
Gothic Art	Surrealism
Greek Art	Symbolism
Impressionism	The Fauves
Indian Art	The Viennese Secession

9 781683 259374